TOILS AND TRIUMPHS

OF

Union Missionary Colportage,

FOR

TWENTY-FIVE YEARS.

BY ONE OF THE SECRETARIES
OF THE AMERICAN TRACT SOCIETY.

PUBLISHED BY THE
AMERICAN TRACT SOCIETY,
150 NASSAU-STREET, NEW YORK.

We address in the following pages our brethren in the Ministry and the pastorate, officers in the army of the Lord of hosts, who are eager to discern and prompt to accept whatever scriptural agency shall proffer its aid in their work of subduing the world to Christ; we address church officers and men of benevolent hearts and means who have consecrated themselves and their wealth to the advancement of Christ's kingdom; we address all who love our Lord Jesus Christ and the souls he has redeemed, beseeching each one to extend to the system of Christian effort herein portrayed, such sympathy, prayer and coöperation as, in his judgment, when candidly made up, shall best subserve the cause of our common Lord.

J. M. S.

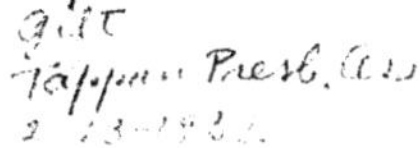

CONTENTS.

CHAPTER VI.

CHAPTER VII.

CONTENTS OF APPENDIX.

COLPORTAGE.

CHAPTER I.

THE SYSTEM DESCRIBED.

In the year 1841 was inaugurated by the officers of the American Tract Society the system of *Union Missionary Colportage*, they little imagining whereunto it would grow. Having completed its quarter of a century, we come to speak of its toils and triumphs, and commend its further prosecution and wide expansion to the attention of the church universal.

The spirit of colportage is found in apostolic times, when the disciples, "who were scattered abroad, went everywhere preaching the word." The name *colporteur*, of French origin, was at an early day applied to the bearer of religious books from house to house, combating error, and talking with the people of the great salvation. In the Reformation, "Germany was overrun with colporteurs," and Luther's works were thus circulated in France, Spain, England, and Italy.

In more recent times the term describes a large class of laborers in Europe who are diffusing the Bible and other books, by sale or gift, among the masses of the people. Its present form in our country was given it in the spring of 1841. For some years previous to this date the American Tract Society had prosecuted with large success the volume enterprise and tract distribution, during which, with the aid of above thirty thousand voluntary laborers, two million volumes of evangelical truth were put into circulation, largely in the cities, chief towns, and wealthy neighborhoods. This effort brought out the fact that immense numbers of our population, and they the most needy, could not be reached by this effort, and hence that some benevolent scheme must be devised for carrying to their houses the word of life.

At this juncture, while the tear of compassion was falling over the neglected millions of the land, and the executive officers were anxiously inquiring what could be done, the agent for volume circulation at the West, Mr. Seely Wood, one of the first and most energetic laborers in the work, came to the anniversary, and spread before the Committee the immense population unreached by the agencies of the Society on his field. "Will the Christian public sustain the men sent out to visit the destitute and dying masses?" was the question anxiously canvassed by the executive officers, Hallock, Eastman, and Cook, Mr. Wood, and others. During protracted conferences, in which the senior Secretary with special earnestness insisted that the destitute masses must be sought out at their own homes, it was at length determined to inaugurate the work, the Committee throwing itself in faith upon the benevolence of the churches. Secretary Cook attended the anniversary of the Society in Boston a few days thereafter, and there publicly presented the scheme, when two men immediately proposed to go out as colporteurs, and a patron appeared to sustain one of them. Thus was originated *Union Missionary Colportage,* to which Mr. Cook gave for many years the best powers of his gifted mind. At the close of the first year, eleven colporteurs had been commissioned; at the end of the second, 23; the succeeding year, 76; the next, 143; the next, 175. And thus the work has advanced till the present.

Colportage, as an evangelizing agency, combines the two great elements of power God has given his people—*the living voice and the living press.* By these, as instruments, singly or united, all advancement, intellectual, social, and religious, is made. The voice is more potent for the moment, the press abiding for the long years. The voice arouses and instructs the worshipping congregations; the press seeks out and warns the larger masses, who rarely go into worshipping assemblies: the voice thrills the thousands gathered upon some great emergency; the press reaches with a quieter power the millions scattered over the land: the voice is limited in its reach; the press ubiquitous in its range. The two combined—the voice uttering burning thoughts, impelled by glowing affections; the press, driven by steam and aided by electricity, multiplying in million-form the truths to be taught—sometimes move our entire people, as the forest is swayed by the winds of heaven.

The combination of these in colportage is most felicitous. A living man, with heart of love and tongue of zeal, and laden with precious pungent printed truth, goes to his field purposing to bring that truth into direct contact with every soul. This he does by seeing the people house by house, individual by individual, conversing of Christ with each, and so far as possible and expedient, praying with all; and when his words of instruction, comfort, warning, or exhortation, have been spoken, his printed truth in the form of tract or book remains to plead for God when he has passed on, each family supplied with words whereby they may be saved. His words wake attention and start inquiry; the books fix the thought and give the information; the personal interview conciliates, the printed volume instructs; the kindness of a Christian visit wins the confidence, the pungency of the tract touches the heart; the prayer in the

Christless cabin sets the children upon wondering inquiry; the picture cards and catechisms placed in their hands explain the duty and blessedness of piety; the exhortation in the social meeting leads Christians to ask, How can we serve God more faithfully? the volumes they secure suggest modes of active good doing; the address to the Sabbath-school awakens new thoughts; the library furnished is a permanent source of interest and instruction.

Colportage is not book-peddling, either in aim, spirit, or result. Its aim, to supply the destitute with saving truth, and bring souls to Christ; its spirit, that of the Master, self-denying and benevolent; its result, the winning of many to the Saviour—all distinguish it broadly from mere book-selling. Nor is it simply a zealous running to and fro in earnest exhortations, much of which is forgotten as soon as uttered, for it places permanent ministers of truth in each house, to urge and reiterate the claims of Christ upon every soul. It is thus seen to be a combination in happy measure of the two world-moving instrumentalities—personal influence and printed truth.

It is called *missionary colportage,* because it *carries its message to the destitute people,* not waiting for them to come after it. Seeking them out in the by-ways and alleys of the city, in the secluded nooks and glens of the country, in the recesses of the forests, in the fastnesses of the mountains, in the wide prairies of the west, in the broad savannahs and dark swamps of the south: wherever human habitations are found or human beings live, there are its footsteps directed and its burdens of truth borne. While it neglects none who may desire and welcome its visits, its chosen field is the destitute—those unreached by other means. As the advanced cohort of the Lord's workers, it sows the seed in all vacant fields, bestows its culture upon all waste places, as the church of Christ should ever work, assured that the local organizations will, one or another, gather the fruitage.

The term *union* missionary colportage expresses the coöperation of evangelical Christians of all names, and the catholicity of its publications and laborers, as distinguished from denominational works and workers.

The fundamental truths of the gospel centring in the cross and clustering about it, are common to the evangelical church in all ages and all lands. This "common salvation," as inspiration terms it, this truth essential to salvation, this "faith of the saints" in all ages, is the principal element in all gospel preaching, the body of the practical and devotional literature of the church, and the truth which the Spirit usually employs in the conversion and sanctification of men. This is the truth which *union* colportage carries to the people.

The colporteurs must also be of catholic spirit, aiming at the one vital point, the union of men to Christ by faith, not unduly influencing their denominational relations.

Such then is the nature of the system: as *colportage*, carrying the good news to the people; as *missionary*, seeking out the specially needy; as *union*, employing the central doctrines in which the church in general unite—combining the use of spoken and printed truth.

CHAPTER II.

THE TRUE PLACE OF THIS UNION AGENCY.

If the church of Christ were a visible and harmonious unit, none could doubt the place and power of a general colportage in the evangelization of the world. The entire body of Christ's people throwing their energies into such a plan for reaching the masses, one generation would scarcely pass until all in civilized lands should hear the blessed name. But we are far from realizing that ideal church in our day. God's children are grouped in many organizations under different names, often in seeming opposition to the real unity; and as each branch of the one true church has modes of Christian effort, boards of missions, education, and publication, a serious question exists in some minds as to coöperating in a union work. The question assumes this shape, "As my own branch of the church is fully organized for the work of Christ, should I not work only in her channels? Is not my highest obligation and first duty to my own denomination? Or may I, in the present divided state of the visible church, wisely expend part of my time and means in a union enterprise?"

While we would not assume to judge for others, the following considerations may aid in reaching a right conclusion.

1. The Christian sustains a precious and cherished relationship to his own section of the church. By voluntary covenant he has entered into this relation, and taken upon himself its vows. He has associated with a little band of the great family, because he in some respects is more nearly allied to them in doctrines, modes of worship, tastes, and general sympathies. With these he labors in supporting the ministry, maintaining public, social, and Sabbath-school services. Here he brings his children to hear the gospel; here he celebrates the love of Christ at His table; and when he dies, here his brethren assemble to lay away his body and mingle their tears with those of his weeping family.

Clearly he owes high and important duties to this particular organization; and if it be a part of a general denomination, his obligations extend to all the members of that section of the church, because of his connection with this local organization. He is not generally the most devoted Christian who has no denominational preferences and attachments. Many duties are best performed in denominational channels, as making a public profession of religion, organizing local churches, attendance regularly upon divine service, educating men for the ministry, and whatever pertains directly to denominational church extension, either at home or abroad.

So far there can be no question. But more may be stated. When his particular branch of the church has wisely undertaken aggressions upon the kingdom of darkness by new organizations, he is bound to give means and time and prayer to aid in this form of effort, for thus will his own denomination, which he believes nearest the scriptural standard, be strengthened and extended.

2. But this Christian is also a member of the church catholic, that grand and glorious body to which the promises of a universal dominion are given. To this blood-bought church—the entire body of Christ—he owes

fraternal affection, kindness, gentleness, loving sympathy, and wherever possible, cordial coöperation. No duty to a local organization or a given denomination can free him from obligation to the church general. He cannot owe an exclusive affection to a fractional part of the one body. As a brother may not love one brother in the family to the injury or even the neglect of others, neither may the members of a particular Christian household so love their restricted circle as to withhold enlarged affection from the whole brotherhood. If, through the imperfection of its members in knowledge and holiness, this one church now appears in a great number of visible parts, its essential unity still exists. "The unity of the church does not require," says one, "absolute uniformity, but admits of many semblances of diversity. She may exist in separated generations, in separate countries, under different names, and in great variety of age, education, taste, and social position, in the same congregation, without destroying her real unity, just as the human race exists in different countries under different forms of government, and in various social conditions, and still is one. A common humanity pervades the race, and links together successive generations, its tides ebbing and flowing in the heart of every man. So amid the differences of true Christians there beats in all hearts a common love for Christ," and, where not repressed and chilled by ignorance, prejudice, or bigotry, for each other. The points in which Christians agree are far more vital than those in which they differ. They constitute one body, are indwelt by one Spirit, have one hope, bow to one Lord, believe in one creed as to the essentials of salvation, have one baptism, by which they are united to Christ, and are all children of one Father. Eph. 4:4–6. "Thus united by a seven-fold bond—essentially a unit—men of different denominations often bow together before the same mercy-seat, and sing the praises of the same Redeemer with one heart in sweet and full accord. Even widely separated generations of Christians have fellowship with each other. The words of a golden-tongued Chrysostom, of a noble Augustine, of a pious Thomas à Kempis, the recorded faith and prayers and hymns of the whole church of the past, refresh the church of the present. Yes, there is a profound unity amid the greatest circumstantial diversity of true Christians. The cry of the anxious soul, 'Men, brethren, what shall we do?' will arouse the pious effort of the Christian as promptly as the cry of the drowning man arouses the humane efforts of him who hears it, and this always and everywhere."

To this church, the whole body of Christ, each member owes an unceasing and wide-reaching affection, which no local organization or single denomination may monopolize; for is not the body worthy of an intenser and more controlling affection than a single one of its members?

3. The strength of this claim will be more impressively felt if we note the Christian's deeply personal relation to Christ, the head of his body, the church universal. By faith he has become one with Christ, and holds constant and sweet communion with him. All his duties arise primarily out of this personal relation, and here lie the motive and mainspring of all his acts. He reads the

Bible because Christ speaks to him in it; he prays in the closet, family, and social meeting, that he may commune with Christ; he restrains evil passions and propensities for Christ's sake; he trains his family in scriptural knowledge that they may learn of Christ; he pleads with sinners to come to Christ. All this he does because he is a Christian. As a minister of the gospel, he preaches because called of God to this work, and not because he belongs to a particular section of the church. The place in which he proclaims the message is determined by his denominational bonds, the message by Christian bonds. Indeed there are few acts of a Christian minister which are primarily denominational. Nine sermons of ten are upon the great themes common to the true church, and would be as appropriate and acceptable in any other evangelical pulpit as in his own. His daily life and personal influence, the sum of his Christian conduct, as that of private members, spring primarily and purely out of his relation to Christ as a redeemed sinner, whereas his external denominational relationships are of far less vital importance.

Here then is the Christian sustaining a cherished relation to his own denomination, and a broader and profounder one to the church universal, both springing out of his personal union to, and identification with, Christ. From which it would appear that his highest duty is directly and personally to his Saviour, then to his whole body the church, and then to that section of the church of which he is a member. In serving Christ, he may neither allow an indiscriminating catholicity to destroy local affection, nor a denominational exclusiveness to forget all except his own narrow circle; but with an affection world-wide and Christ-like, he must labor in those channels in which, guided by an enlightened and scriptural judgment, he may best promote the glory of Christ and the unity of his visible church.

While a part of his Christian effort should be in denominational channels, shall it all be thus expended? Is there no broader field where, joining hands with brethren of other names, members with him of the one glorious church, he may do a grand work, which, in his denominational capacity, owing to the divisions in Christ's body, he cannot so speedily and efficiently perform? May it not be that the different denominations, clustering at the centres of population, in efforts to establish local churches, leave large numbers of the outlying and interlying masses unsupplied with gospel privileges, which some union effort of good men may reach?

If it shall appear that at least one-third of our entire population are, and must continue for long years, beyond the direct range of the denominational organizations, is it not at least possible that they may be overtaken more speedily by some combined agency? If we cannot immediately supply them with the full equipment of gospel ordinances, may we not carry to them the Bible and the "common salvation," in which we all agree, and press upon them, with earnest pleas from loving hearts, the claims of a common Saviour?

This form of inquiry we beg to press upon the attention of ministers and office-bearers in every branch of the evangelical church. If all work for Christ must be done in denominational channels, then is there no need or place for Bible Societies, Tract Societies, or union colportage. It is possible for Christians to labor exclusively in their own section of the church, to confine their benefactions, sympathies, and even prayers to their own denomination, and to refuse fraternal intercourse with all but the narrowest circle; or, retaining firmly their visible church connection, their ministry, their sacraments, their creeds and catechisms, their schools and colleges and missionary boards, they may yet heartily and efficiently coöperate with brethren of other names in a union effort to reach speedily with the offer of salvation the outlying and perishing masses. Which plan they should pursue is a question of vital import.

If it shall appear that such a coöperative work as *union missionary colportage* comes to the captious and the unbelieving with special power, disarming them of prejudice and winning their confidence by a sole desire to bring them to a loving Saviour, this will constitute an urgent reason for enlisting in its support.

Further, if the heart of the church universal has ever sought for some public expression of its oneness, has striven after it with a desire so ardent as almost to accept as scriptural the forced and unnatural semblance of unity seen in the Romish system, may there not be some organizations, embracing thousands of the good men of every evangelical name, who will give, in their union work for Christ, an impressive exhibition of the true spiritual oneness of the body of Christ—a union of faith in the essential truths, a union of affection in Christian offices, a union of effort in works of evangelization?

Such an expression of Christian unity—unity in doctrine, in affection, in labor—is the system of *union missionary colportage* as originated and prosecuted by the American Tract Society. During twenty-five years, above four thousand laborers of various denominations have been engaged in this blessed coöperation, have made millions of Christian visits to the needy, speaking only of salvation through the Redeemer, and have circulated many millions of books and tracts, all containing the admitted truths of the "common salvation." And to aid in carrying forward this work, unnumbered men and women have contributed their means. sympathies, and prayers. May it not well be called the *practical evangelical alliance* for the conversion of the unreached masses?

That there is urgent need for such coöperative work, that it can be done without infringing upon the prerogatives of any denomination, and that it may be performed to the great advantage of the true church of our Lord, we think may be conclusively shown.

CHAPTER III.

THE NEED OF SUCH AN AGENCY.

A COMBINATION of causes creates a necessity for some such agency. The wide expanse of our country opening new fields for emigration and enterprise; the sudden development of new forms of labor and wealth, as seen in the mining and oil regions; the inflow weekly of thousands from other countries; the abounding facilities for travel in all directions; and the general prosperity of all classes, with immense increase of national wealth, create and foster a ceaseless migration of our people. Thousands are removing from old homes to new, and this through all the years. The stream flowing Westward is vast and resistless, and as it approaches the great basin, spreads out like the channels of the Nile or the Mississippi, pouring its multitudes by millions into new and diverse localities. In addition, war has recently desolated one-third of our states, breaking up their system of labor, sweeping away their wealth, and creating millions of freemen without homes or an assured resting-place.

As the result of these and like causes, above one-third of our population are destitute of the means of grace as furnished in church organizations; in some places one-fourth, in others one-third, in still others more than the half have no accessible house of evangelical worship. And herein lies the need of a union colportage which shall be able, adapting itself to the actual destitutions in any locality, to reach every soul with the word of life.

If the church were a single organization, holding her power in hand for every exigency, fired with a great love for souls, and ready to project a new congregation wherever a new cluster of houses appeared, she might overtake and supply these destitutions by a united effort. As now constituted, she attempts to push out into the waste places—a half-dozen systems of denominational organizations, interlacing and overlapping each other in village, and hamlet, and neighborhood, where there is scarce material enough for one; hence great numbers in the more sparsely settled regions must be unreached. This does not imply want of energy in the different sections of the church, but loss of power from want of union.

It seems impossible for those who have not explored portions of the country in order to learn the facts, to believe the extent of this destitution, and that it exists, in measure, everywhere. Colportage, as an exploring agency, has, by its laborers running to and fro for twenty-five years, accumulated a mass of testimony upon this point from which there is no escape—the destitution *is vast, ubiquitous, fearful.* Cases of want found and met with blessed results crowd upon us.

In the New England states we see common schools, Sabbath-schools, churches, and an intelligent, educated people, where we might not expect to find much need of such missionary labor. Nowhere in our land, perhaps, is there such a general supply of gospel ordinances; and yet even here have been found very many unreached by the means of grace. A clerical colporteur, who has labored for two years in Maine and northern New Hampshire, says, "I find many dark and neglected corners, where the families are reached by no other agency. They have no Sabbath-school, attend no religious meeting, are not known by the resident ministers, each supposing they fall within the care of others. They themselves are restrained by unreasonable prejudices, chained down by poverty, or stupefied by unbelief. Many towns have these dark borders, into which the rays of religious truth seldom shine. In one town I found forty families without any religious book, several without the Bible, though it contained three evangelical churches." Another in a different portion of New England avers of his field, "Not more than one-fourth of the population attend upon preaching of any kind. Many professed Christians seem more devoted to the service of the world than of Christ. Many towns are destitute of the stated means of grace; intemperance and kindred sins prevail to an alarming extent, and Christian home-training is greatly neglected." With modifications, this is true of portions of every New England state.

Passing to New York, we find the same truth constantly presented, the result of careful examination. One colporteur testifies: "Nearly or quite one-third of the people on my field are unreached by ministers, and unvisited by Christian laymen, and unless sought out by the colporteur, must live and die unwarned and uncared for." Another avers: "The voluntary destitution of many is amazing. Here is a family, living near a large village where are Bibles, and good books, and a church, who had not possessed a Bible for nineteen years, nor been to a religious meeting for several years. Here is another, father, mother, and seven children. He has kept house eleven years without a Bible, and in neglect of the sanctuary." Still another speaks of a mother and three children, with whom he prayed. "On rising from my knees, I found them in tears, the mother saying, by way of apology, they never heard any one pray before, and knew not what it meant. And that family lived within the sound of church bells, though she admitted they had not been to church in nine years."

This truth becomes painfully impressive as we pass into the Middle states, increasingly so the farther we go, following the onrushing of population. "In one of these counties more than half the territory is destitute of a religious teacher." "One lady told me she had not been to meeting for six years, another for two, another for eight." "In a district twenty-four miles long and fifteen broad, there is neither stated preaching nor Sabbath-school." "In a village of twelve hundred souls, not above one-fourth attend the sanctuary."

Facts from the Western states are still more distressing. A pastor in Michigan gives this fact: "There are 2,200 souls in this new county, 300 of whom are connected with the churches, 400 more may occasionally attend preaching leaving 1,500 without any means of grace." Over scores of counties of the vast Northwest equal destitutions exist. The evidence is overwhelming.

Turning our eyes Southward, with a pitying glance, over eleven states lately swept by mighty armies, filled with widows and orphans, impoverished by loss of men, material, and labor; with churches destroyed, congregations scattered, schools broken up, and struggling under accumulated evils, can we expect any thing better than widespread and most fearful destitutions? The seven following sentences, from as many different letters, present a sad view: "Nearly half the families I visited were destitute of religious reading." "One village has neither church nor school-house within three miles, and there is but one professor of religion in it." "I have been in many places where the gospel trumpet was never sounded, nor a prayer ever heard by many of the young." "Many counties in this state are without a church, minister, Sabbath-school, or common-school." "Unless the colporteur take good books to these families and talk to them of Jesus, many will grow up and never hear His name." "The people have no religious books, no Bibles, no preaching; colportage alone will reach them." "Not more than one-third of the people are supplied with regular preaching, and not more than one-third of these attend."

A colporteur in Tennessee says: "My field embraces two counties, with a population of twenty thousand souls, who, even before the war, were without a bookstore, and had but seven educated ministers. Multitudes hear the gospel but once a month, and many never. I found seven families on one mountain, thirty upon another, and twenty-seven upon a third, entirely separated from all good influences." A minister of high standing from another point writes: "Since the war, religion and morals have fallen into a deplorable condition; churches are without pastors, houses of worship wholly destroyed or unused. God is greatly forgotten; his name much profaned. Wrath and malice, bitterness and revenge, lurk and brood in many hearts that are estranged from each other. Vice and crime are prevalent. What but the saving grace of God can recover us from this unhappy state?"

A minister in Texas, perhaps better acquainted than any other man with the religious condition of its people, after giving a sad picture of the wants of the freedmen and the poor white people, makes the following startling statement: "Besides Americans, there are fifty thousand Germans in the state, of whom five thousand are Roman-catholics. Not above two thousand of this number attend regularly upon the gospel ministry, leaving forty-eight thousand souls which, if not reached through the faithful colporteur, may be left to perish." Such is the unsolicited testimony of a trustworthy man.

The destitutions throughout the entire Southern states, with few exceptions, are fearful beyond description, as the result in part of the protracted and desolating strife. Including the entire population, we cannot hope that one half of them have any adequate gospel privileges. Millions upon millions are perishing now for want of the bread of life, and must perish eternally unless the true church of God, North and South, shall work with a sterner purpose and a more flaming zeal than she has ever yet done.

But why give isolated examples of the need? The general result of facts which have been accumulated during many years, and by four thousand laborers, in this field of effort, confirmed by the investigations of other societies and individuals, is that *more than one-third of our entire population are unreached by the organized churches.*

Is there not, then, an imperative call for some agency with capabilities equal to the demand, and adaptations suited to the exigency? Some system so extensive as to reach the ten millions of our population now unreached by the organized churches; so versatile as to meet each case; so evangelical as to present saving truth; so earnest, prayerful, persevering, and believing, as to secure the blessing of God?

CHAPTER IV.

SPECIAL ADAPTATION.

HAS Union Missionary Colportage any special aptitude to meet this want?

Denominational colportage is clearly adapted to meet the wants of its own people. A given branch of the visible church, having adopted a system of doctrine and mode of worship which it believes most nearly conformed to the teachings of the Bible, desires to use the press in aid of the ministry, for indoctrinating all its members and families in the truths believed and forms of worship practised. To accomplish this it must first create a denominational literature adapted to all classes of its people, and this in great variety of form to meet the varying shades of thought, taste, and mental development, of its congregations.

This accomplished, it remains to convey this truth to the families of its people, and press it upon their attention and actual acceptance by sale or gift. In the pressure of exhausting labor now exacted of the ministry, it should not be asked of them to do this needed work; nor should we wait for the people to come for these publications. Here denominational colportage stands ready for the toil. Let energetic men, who feel it important to train up the churches in their belief and practice, be chosen and freighted with the volumes and tracts prepared, and sent into all the local organizations of that denomination. Let the pastor furnish the names and residences of all the membership, and let the poorest and most ignorant be sought and supplied freely with this denominational and other literature, and let this system be carried on from year to year, and a vast increase of intelligent and scripturally indoctrinated church membership may be expected as the result. The system can be extended as the denomination enlarges, and adapted to the wants of that branch of the church. So might each denomination prepare and circulate a literature suited to its distinguishing doctrines, and thus every branch of the evangelical church train its own families.

But in the meantime, the years—ages, it may be—before this shall come, how shall the millions interlying and outlying beyond the influence of the evangelical denominations be visited and supplied with the central truths in which they all agree? the soul-saving truths without which they must be lost? the foundation truths which, accepted, will fit them for membership in any one of the denominations?

That Union Colportage has the most felicitous adaptation to this unreached population, is readily seen. A literature embodying the essential doctrines, and avoiding minor controverted points, has been in the course of preparation for forty years. It has accomplished the vast accumulation of three thousand five hundred distinct books, from the entire Bible with references, maps, notes, and instructions, and numerous Bible helps, down to the picture card and the infant catechism, covering a wide field of practical, devotional, revival, biographical, historical, and critical writings; each of which works is, as far as possible, permeated and suffused with the Spirit, and love, and holiness of Christ; all variations, rich, and sweet, and soul-moving, upon the one key-note, "Christ, and him crucified."

Here, then, is the first requisite for union colportage—the stores of generally-admitted truth. Can the second be secured? Can devoted Christian men be found in the different denominations, of scriptural knowledge, irreproachable character, burning zeal, unquestioned prudence, untiring perseverance, and Christlike self-sacrifice, who, while retaining their own denominational preferences, will yet consent to hold these in abeyance, urging only the "common salvation," as they go forth among the gospel neglecters? To this question the experience of twenty-five years, and the actual employment of above four thousand men by the American Tract Society, give the decisive answer. In every denomination of the true Israel such men have been, will be found.

Freight these men with this literature, and bid them go forth into the highways and hedges of our entire country, to the one-third of the people now unreached, and what favor will they meet?

The pastor welcomes union colportage as an illustration of Christian zeal which he longs to see kindled among his own people; as an aid to him in the prayer-meeting and the revival; as a faithful visitor to all the careless gospel neglecters scattered among his people, and upon the outskirts of his congregation; as the tireless seeker out of the children attending no Sabbath-school; in a word, to discover and report gospel delinquents, and if possible, to lead all to some church of Christ. Christian parents welcome him for the blessed effects of his visits upon their children and households. The souls burdened on account of sin, many of whom are found in all religious communities, welcome him because he so freely speaks to them of their concealed griefs, and so plainly and affectionately points them to the great Physician. The careless listen to his exhortations, for they glow with the fervor of an unselfish consecration. The captious and skeptical, who magnify the defects of Christians and their want of agreement among themselves into an unanswerable argument against Christianity; who insist, in exaggerated phrase, that the church is broken up into a hundred fragments, each at war with every other, and make this their great stumbling-block—even these are compelled to admit that union colportage is an illustration of a united church, laboring solely to save men without regard to denominational aggrandizement. So that these laborers are met everywhere and among all classes, either with a joyful welcome, or a willing toleration, which gives them a vast power for good.

It may be well to note this special adaptation of union colportage in several particulars; as first,

To the present divided state of the church. Upon this point it is difficult to present the testimony before us without a liability of being understood as depreciating denominational efforts. Nothing is farther from our purpose; the entire aim being to show the special adaptation of this agency to this class, not its superiority to denominational effort, where there is material for a church organization.

One writer says, "Your publications, free from the peculiarities which mark a sect, are received with almost universal favor." Another: "My field contains at least seventeen denominations. I can, with good faith, approach them all, and give them just what suits them, without being blamed for trying to build up any one. I am welcomed by nearly all, and have aided many in revival meetings, pointing sinners to the Lamb of God, and furnishing better printed instructions than my poor words. When asked what denomination my books belong to, I answer, 'To all and for all; just the books God blesses for leading sinners to him, and building up believers in faith.'"

Another testifies: "I am hailed as coming from a national institution, and greeted as laboring for the good of all, interested only in their spiritual welfare." Another: "As my work is for everybody in need and everywhere, and not for any particular order of Christians, I am welcomed by good people, and rarely repelled by any. Joining the people in their prayer-meetings, as I constantly do, talking and praying as I would do if a member of their own church, helps them to feel more brotherly to other denominations

How many crooked, fault-finding professors are silenced by a kind talk in the spirit of Christ." Another says: "I am often told these are the publications which should be circulated among all classes; they will do good to all, and harm to none. A faithful and highly-esteemed minister said to me, 'If I were going out as a colporteur, I would go from your Society, as I could thus, free from captious objection, speak to any one of Christ;' and so I find it everywhere."

Such is the testimony of hundreds of colporteurs, and in all states of the Union; and this is just what we should expect, human nature being what it is. The excuse of the gospel neglecter, that Christians do not agree among themselves, is not a good one, and usually is a mere subterfuge; still it is universal, and with the unregenerate is, perhaps, one of the most potent. He has repeated it over and over until he believes in its validity, and by a minister of a given denomination it is, he thinks, unanswerable. But a plain, earnest colporteur presses upon him the claims of Christ in what the objector sees is an unselfish wish for his salvation, without regard to any particular church relation; by his life of self-sacrifices he demonstrates that he seeks the souls of men; this disarms opposition, and the objecter often yields.

Adaptation to the common mind. The three thousand five hundred different publications prepared by the Society are nearly all adapted to the comprehension of the common people, the masses of poorly educated and hard working ones, who constitute so large a portion of our population. To furnish these with the marrow of the gospel in cheap editions, in plain language, and with striking illustrations, has been a cherished object of the Society. If men of large intellectual resources and ambitious aspirings after greatness find little to interest them in these publications, the godly minister, laboring to win souls to the Saviour, turns to them as the richest storehouse of saving truth, aiding him in presenting the gospel to the comprehension of the untrained masses.

Colportage usually chooses its laborers from the ranks of the common people, selecting those who, by years of experience in the Christian life, by special devotion to the cause of the Master, by native talent for conversation, and acquired readiness in prayer, are fitted for commending to the people the religion they have experienced; men inured to hardness as good soldiers, able to endure the toils, the coarse fare, the poor lodgings, the rough habits of too many in our land; men who can therefore place themselves in sympathy with the common people, win their confidence, interest their minds, sympathize in their lot, and lead them to higher aspirations. The entire history of the work has shown its adaptation to this result.

A faithful Christian pastor who has devoted thirty-five years to evangelizing efforts in the West, acting as a voluntary colporteur over wide fields before the work had been reduced to a system, and ever since, after giving illustrations of its power in the conversion of souls, as witnessed by him, adds these words: "I admire this work as without an equal in one aspect—that its agencies are so happily adapted to the common mind. We do not estimate aright the power of strong, striking, self-sealing thoughts on minds unused to think, but which to the intelligent are familiar as the alphabet. This is what gave such a charm to the teachings of Jesus. He originated bold thoughts, delivered them in simple language, and gathered his pictures from scenes which were to his countrymen familiar as household words; and we are not surprised that the common people heard him gladly, followed him into the desert and around the lake, wondering at the gracious words he uttered."

The value of any system adapted to the common people will be appreciated when we consider that four-fifths or more of our destitute come under this appellation.

Adaptation to the very poor and destitute. Any system which will accomplish what is needed in our country to-day must have a penetrating power to reach the poorest, most secluded, most destitute. Churches will be organized by one or another denomination wherever villages, or even thickly-settled neighborhoods are found; but many thousands of our people have wandered far from the centres of population, many live isolated, and not a few of these are both ignorant and poor. To these the gospel should be preached—must be, if we obey the command of our risen Lord. But thousands of these will pass into eternity unwarned, unless an itinerant and all-pervasive agency shall seek them out in their isolation, and supply their crying wants. This, missionary colportage is exactly adapted to accomplish. None too poor to be visited, and prayed with, and exhorted to higher aspirations; none so destitute that they cannot be supplied. Of the mountainous parts of New Jersey, a colporteur writes: "Many families cannot attend any church, and they are destitute of all saving influences. They are perishing for want of spiritual food. Oh that Christians could be aroused to the importance of seeking and saving these dying ones."

In the forests of New York, a laborer testifies: "I left my horse, and went a few miles into the woods to find some families remote from gospel means. I was depressed in spirit in view of the character which they were reputed to have, and knelt by a log and committed my way to my blessed Saviour. The first man I found was without love to Christ. He promised that his wife should read to him the little books I gave—he could not read. I went to another clearing, and found a number of men at work. They were all strangers to grace. One of them kindly went with me through the brush to find a path to another house. Of nine families thus found that day, most of them without the Bible or any good book, I conversed and prayed with seven. Several said no one had ever before talked to them about the welfare of their souls. Another day I sought out eight poor families, conversed on personal religion with five of them. Four of them had not a scrap of religious reading; five were without the Bible. I supplied them all. Still another tour revealed ten families utterly destitute of religion; among them, a woman with four ragged children, in the deepest poverty, who yet, when I spoke of the love of Christ, burst into tears, and said she often felt the need of a new heart, that she might love him. These poor people must be sought out, or they will perish."

A clerical colporteur, laboring in Delaware, was impressed with the numbers of utterly desolate ones who were unreached by the regular means of grace, and among many cases met almost daily, he cites this: "I found a miserably poor widow with five children, the eldest thirteen years of age, living in a log hut, the door without hinges, no glass in the window, the light and wind coming in between the logs, the roof leaking, and but one bed in which she and her five children slept—a picture of deepest poverty. Her eyes filled with tears as she spoke of her trials. As neither she nor the children could read, except the eldest a very little, I gathered them about me, and told them of the way of life, and left some simple stories which the child might spell out, and perhaps understand. Who will carry the bread of life to these desolate ones?"

A godly worker in Virginia gives even a sadder view of the poor on his field: "One lady, a Christian, once rich, wept bitterly when I called, saying, 'My children are growing up without a knowledge of Christ. We have no preaching, and I have no means to purchase good books.'" He adds: "There are over two hundred families in this county without Bible, Testament, or religious book, and without means to purchase. There are many widows and orphans who must have something to point them to the Lamb of God; and the colporteur is the only one who can meet their wants just now, as many of them cannot afford sufficient clothing to appear in a congregation, and all the means of grace they can enjoy must be carried to their houses."

To such cases as these, and they are fearfully numerous, colportage goes as an angel of mercy, with light, and love, and sweet comfort, in its message. To its efficiency, a minister testifies: "From what my eyes have seen, my ears have heard, my heart has felt, I do not hesitate to regard the system of catholic colportage as the cheapest and best method of which I have any knowledge, to reach, elevate, and evangelize, the destitute millions, found among the mountains, in the wide valleys, and in the ten thousand waste places of our land."

Adaptation to the desolate, sick, and dying. Wearisome days, sleepless nights, and protracted and painful suffering, are allotted to some of God's trusting and patient children;

but when surrounded by kind friends, attended by skilful physicians, and comforted by the counsels and prayers of godly pastors, the sick chamber often becomes a place of heavenly joy. And when death comes to such an abode, he seems robbed of his terrors, and a welcome messenger to take the saint home. But how few of earth's myriads suffer and die thus! How many without hope, and without sympathy, pass away into the dark unknown! No sadder sight does earth produce than is often witnessed by the colporteur in his journeys among the poor. With the same immortal natures with us, the same spiritual needs, the same certainty of a coming judgment, but without the light and comfort of the blessed hope, they struggle with disease, writhe in pain, groan in agony of spirit, and die in despair. If ever the gospel comes as a pure angel of mercy, it is to such agonized souls, to whom no minister of Christ has access. To such, the colporteur often comes just in the hour when the desolate spirit is longing for some one to explain repentance and faith, to tell of Christ's atoning work, of his willingness and ability to save, or to cheer the departing spirit as it enters the dark valley.

In the mountains of Virginia, a colporteur had sought out the isolated dwellers, and told them of the Saviour. Seven years later, in revisiting that field, he was called to the cabin of a dying woman, who addressed him thus: "You were the messenger of mercy to me, and I wish you to be present when I die." She lingered some hours, hearing his counsels and responding to his petitions, gaining faith for the final scene, and then said to her husband, "John, I am going to glory. I will stay till you come, and will look for you every day;" and so departed in the faith, having learned of the way only through the humble colporteur. So poor was the family, and so far removed from "the settlement," that this rescued and now glorified one was wrapped in a sheet and laid away in a coffin made of boards hewn out of the timber by her own sons after her death.

Adaptation to those speaking foreign tongues. Assuredly, one of the most difficult problems before the American churches is this, How shall we reach effectively, with the gospel of Christ, immigrants, of whom a thousand per day are seeking our shores from the nations of the old world? They will be permanent members of society and citizens of the state, bearing their proportion of its burdens, and having an equal share in its management; and they now constitute a powerful element in determining the future of our social, political, and religious character. They speak all the tongues of Europe, and are of all shades of belief, with a large prevalence of Romish tendencies, or of blank infidelity. With such a population, amounting to one-fourth, perhaps, of our entire people, it is evident that their assimilation to our institutions, and above all their speedy evangelization, are of vital moment to our future well-being as a nation.

Colportage has demonstrated its adaptation, in a most felicitous manner, and to a remarkable degree, to this needed work. By its many-tongued colporteurs—and men have been employed speaking three, four, and five languages—and by its books and tracts in the nine leading languages of these thousands, it can reach almost every soul with the truth of Christ. The success of the work in this nearly unoccupied field would justify its enlargement tenfold. We simply advert to this vast field without giving illustrations.

CHAPTER V.

THE VERSATILITY OF COLPORTAGE.

In a new country, where society is in a forming process, and agricultural and mechanical skill is scarce, he is a useful man who can "turn his hand" to any thing which needs to be done. In like manner the moral and religious agencies which would keep abreast of the wants of our rapidly changing people, must have much of this versatile power, promptly adapting themselves to the ever-varying phases of society. Colportage is characterized by this versatility to an almost unlimited extent, illustrations of which press for record.

In time of war. When the fearful scourge of war came upon us, calling out hundreds of thousands from their homes and churches, crowding them into camps, cutting them off from social, intellectual, and Christian privileges, and exposing them to new and violent temptations, it was impossible for the church through denominational channels to meet this new emergency; but union colportage stood ready, and instantly entered upon the work. The first regiment passing through New York in April, 1861, on its way to save Washington, was met and supplied with religious reading; and the last army in the field was supplied in like manner; while all the way through the bloody strife godly men were found in every department, employing the double agency of the voice and the press to hold back the soldiery from sin and bring them to the cross. This work, commenced by the Tract Society, and followed by others, soon developed itself on a grand scale in the United States Christian Commission, which, in its almost limitless range of ministry, was but a specific application of union colportage to this new and vast demand. The details of that work, as conducted by the Commission, do not fall within our range. As conducted by the American Tract Society, they are already written upon many hundred pages of its reports, and their hallowed effects upon many thousand hearts; and the facts demonstrate indubitably the adaptation of the agency to the end sought.

A long-time laborer in a western state wrote from its capital, where the soldiers were collected in large numbers at the beginning of the war, "What a field is opened in the camps! I was the first to commence religious services among them on the Sabbath, and continued them with the assistance of the pastors, until a chaplain was appointed. I also organized prayer-meetings, blessed to many, as I have since learned."

The experiences of one of the Society's colporteurs in a southern state, and the good use to which his books were put, are well told by him: "The confederate authorities seized all my books, and appropriated them for the reading of their army. As the judge knew me, he gave the books to me to distribute. I immediately went into the army, and commenced my work, and with good effect, for a revival of religion soon was spreading through the ranks, and several young men told me the reading of these publications was the means of their coming to the Saviour. One sad result followed. When the federal forces came to my house, the commanding officer learned that I had been in the Confederate army—he knew not in what capacity—and he put me under arrest, and allowed the foragers to strip my house of provisions, wardrobe, and every thing; I saw my poor family reduced to beggary, and I was in the hands of the military. I was driven to despair, when my wife—God bless the woman—thought of my commission from the American Tract Society. She handed it to the commanding officer, whose headquarters were at my house. After examining it, he called for me and asked, "Have you been a colporteur for this Society?" "Yes, sir, for six years, and rejoice in it." "Well, sir, if I had known this, not a thing should have been taken from you. You are discharged from custody, sir." After this I could generally make the commission a sure protection.

On another occasion, army colporteur John E. Vassar, when following the army of the Potomac and laboring for the good of the soldiers, was captured by the cavalry of Gen. Lee, near Gettysburg. Not appearing with military garb and equipment, he was suspected as a spy, charged, and about to be tried, with excitement running high against him, when he thought of his commission, and produced it. His captors instantly relaxed their stern visages, commended his work, took his word of honor not to leave his present position for six hours, and bade him go free.

The commission of the Society was a sure passport to the camps of the soldiery in all places and at all times. The army colporteurs could go wherever a squad of soldiers could penetrate. In the peaceful camp, in the forced march, in the deadly charge, in the disastrous retreat, in the beleagured fort, in the long-drawn trenches, in the open battle-field, and in the crowded hospital, they were found swift to aid the wounded, sick, or dying; and no brighter page is written in the history of humane and Christian effort than that which tells of Union Colportage through the Sanitary and Christian commissions, and by the agents of this Society. Details, abundant and cheering, are on record.

To Seamen. Not less adapted is Union Colportage to the wants and circumstances of sailors, seamen, and boatmen, in our navy, merchant marine, and on our rivers, lakes, and canals. These classes comprise some hundreds of thousands of men, cut off, by their occupation, from church, and home, and the refining influences of female society, and exposed to many demoralizing tendencies. They greatly need some expression of the Christian heart of the land, which shall reach them in their isolation, and tell them, in an effective form, of the claims of a redeeming Saviour upon their affections and service. This, colportage effects to an extent almost ubiquitous in its range, and with just such counsels and publications as reach their minds and hearts. At the different seaports, most largely at New York, the outgoing vessels are supplied with books and tracts in the various languages represented among seamen; packages are also supplied for distribution in foreign ports, and upon the return voyages. On our lakes, rivers, and canals, through seamen's societies, the same work is carried forward unceasingly, and with abounding evidence that God approves. We need not ask whether any other than a union agency could reach with acceptance and promise of usefulness these various and numerous classes. None other attempts the work to any extent, so far as we know. We give a solitary example of what has been done by one man upon a single thoroughfare.

"Since May, 1860, I have been principally engaged in laboring to improve the moral and spiritual condition of the sailors and others who daily pass through the Welland canal. In the second year I was received with the utmost cordiality, which was not invariably the case during my first season. Groups of sailors surrounded me and listened attentively to my pleas for Jesus. They received tracts, and as the result of reading them, I found many under deep conviction, and over some I rejoice as true converts. The general behavior of the boatmen has greatly improved, profanity and drunkenness being much lessened, and increased interest in religious reading exhibited by the sailors. A captain said, 'Sir, you are doing us a great amount of good. My men all read your tracts, and they have ceased visiting the whiskey-shops in consequence. I want a new tract for each man.' I have found many Roman-catholics and infidels glad to receive books and tracts. To a captain of this latter class I sold 'Nelson's Cause and Cure.' When I next met him he said, 'Nelson met my case exactly, and cured me of infidelity.' A captain said, 'You are doing a great amount of good among these men; it can now be conceived only in part.' Another, 'Your work is accomplishing wonders in the lives and conduct of these men.'

"These men are exposed to losses by shipwreck, and they have lonely hours when they have nothing to read. I see no other way of reaching them than by colportage. The colporteur, with his unsectarian principles, can find access to all ranks and classes of society, and offers such books as are approved by all evangelical denominations."

This colporteur has visited six thousand two hundred and twenty-two vessels, and circulated, by sale and grant, $7,500 worth of saving truth during his long and faithful service; but what figures shall tell the amount of good done for the men themselves, their families at home to whom the books finally come, and for all reached by their influence?

To Infidels. That error of all grades, from

mere formalism down to sheer infidelity and blank atheism, abounds in some parts of our land, becomes fearfully apparent to those who employ so pervasive an agency as Missionary Colportage. And the impossibility of reaching it by the ordinary instrumentalities of the denominations, is equally patent. The heretical sects guard their adherents from the influence of the evangelical churches most rigidly; and the skeptics and atheists, of course, avoid the churches where the gospel is truly proclaimed, declaiming, in their hatred of Christ, against what they call "priestcraft and superstition." These classes can only be reached by an agency so aggressive as to go wherever men live, so benevolent as to disarm, or at least assuage the bitterness of prejudice. How happily colportage turns itself to this difficult work is illustrated by instances numerous and striking.

A colporteur in the Northwest, laboring among a people given up to formalism and flagrant error, says, "Though I have not access to these foreigners' pulpits, yet I can take a chair for my pulpit and a family for my audience, and preach Christ and him crucified, and seldom do I have careless hearers. In this way I can reach the Universalist and the Spiritualist. Oh, how they strive to make us give up that old Bible, or pervert it to their notions! How many hundreds there are for miles all around these churches that scarcely hear more than the bell that invites others to worship God." Who will be preacher and Sabbath-school teacher to them at their firesides, but the colporteur?

Another reports some startling facts, showing that the arch-enemy of truth is busily employing this very system of colportage in scattering widely the seeds of ruin and death. He says, "I have visited, during the quarter, five different counties, carrying as many books as I could, and hunting up the people in their shanties and hamlets. One of the greatest enemies I had to contend with was Renan's 'Life of Jesus.' Hearing that, by the liberality of some wealthy infidels, two intelligent agents were canvassing a neighboring county, and selling this dangerous book at a reduced price, I travelled day and night to reach the place to try, by the help of God, to counteract the mischief. Wherever that book was read it seemed to have swept away every true principle of Christianity. I labored to get the start of these wicked men, and succeeded in persuading some pious friends to assist me. We continued for several days, and it pleased the Lord to bless our labors so abundantly that they had to leave the field, as the people would not buy their book when they had seen but a small supply of our good books. They did not, however, leave without a severe struggle; and my labor during that time was one of continued praying, doubting, fearing, and yet hoping. Often have I stood in the midst of a people ignorant of the way of salvation, the victims of those who reject the blood of the covenant and sneer at our glorious religion. Even now as I am writing, the cry for help from thousands of perishing souls is still ringing in my ears. I cannot drive from my sight the horrible vision of a people hurrying to eternal destruction. If Christians would do their duty, many might be saved from infidelity. I am convinced, and have the blessed assurance that this seed, sown with many tears and earnest prayers, will bear fruit, as sure as a Saviour's promises cannot be broken."

To Romanists. No class of errorists is so numerous, and few are so unapproachable as Roman-catholics. In the cities and larger towns, under the constant supervision of the priesthood, but few of them are successfully reached by evangelical influences: in the country, and especially on the outskirts of population, where surrounded by Protestants, they may be brought under the power of the gospel. The antiquity of that system, the amount of truth it professes, and the tact and zeal of its priesthood, give it great power over its honest votaries; while its imposing ceremonies, and gorgeous ritual, and lax morality, adapt it to the tastes and desires of the unrenewed. Yet we cannot doubt that the truth as it is in Jesus is making some headway among them. The prevalence of free inquiry, general education, and the wide diffusion of printed truth, will in time dissipate the ignorance and overthrow the prejudice which are the bulwarks of their system. As an auxiliary in this, colportage has vast power, and has already reaped large rewards, though it is true that much of its labor among Romanists has produced no immediate fruit. But as the simple gospel, presented in an earnest spirit and an uncontroversial form, is mighty through God, we know good will follow in his time.

A colporteur in Nova Scotia testifies that "kind and earnest discussion with Catholics causes them to think and exercise their judgment upon matters that concern their salvation. I sell books largely among them, and sometimes to the priests. To one I sold Baxter and Burder, and two packages of tracts, in which he said he might get some useful hints. A young man bought the Testament with notes, to compare it with their own. By giving them good books, and dealing gently with them in argument, and praying with and for them, I am convinced much good may be done. There is the strongest demand for such labor among them now; for as education advances, and the mind expands from the iron grasp of priestcraft, unless something purer is presented, it will plunge into infidelity. I meet some already carried away."

Sometimes the colporteur "catches them with guile," as did Paul the captious ones of his day. A shrewd laborer overheard a wily Romanist lay a wager that he "could buy a pack of cards of that hypocritical Protestant," and was ready when approached in a confidential tone, and asked if he had "any cards." "Certainly," said the colporteur, "if you will put them quietly in your pocket, and let no one know where you got them." Chuckling over his success, the Romanist paid for the "Scripture" cards, and went home. "Next morning I noticed the children were well supplied with these 'Scripture Facts,' and I tried to meet my *customer*, but he invariably found a cross-street before coming within speaking distance. So, for once, the Tract Society had a Roman-catholic colporteur distributing 'Scripture Facts' among Roman-catholic families."

Another writes that on a part of his field the people are mostly Romanists, among whom, especially upon his second and subsequent visits, he sold and granted many books and tracts, and with some he enjoyed precious seasons of prayer.

Another describes a timely visit to a lady who was to have been baptized on the following Sabbath by the priest, but who bought of him some books, one of which was "Nevins' Thoughts on Popery," and was rescued. "She often thanks God that I came just at that crisis. Those books opened her eyes; though my door was well pounded with brickbats for the good act of delivering her out of their hands."

But we need not insist further upon the versatility of this agency, by which it can adapt itself to every state of society, and meet every possible exigency. A shrewd man, with a warm Christian heart, with ready utterance and a thorough knowledge of human nature, and withal supplied with the widest range of practical and scriptural books and many hundred different tracts, can scarcely ever be taken at unawares; nor will he find a human being whose moral and spiritual condition demand counsel or instruction which his stores are not adapted to meet. "I find this great advantage," writes an experienced colporteur, "that while my work is purely evangelical, it is not denominational. I can reach all; and prejudice is disarmed. I introduce the subject of religion in each house, and have constant opportunities for instruction, warning, and exhortation. Admonitions coming unexpectedly from a *book peddler*, as they at first regard me, often, with the blessing of God, make a deeper impression because they were unlooked-for. A lady once said to me, 'I envy you your opportunities for doing good. The very titles of your books and tracts introduce for you the subject of salvation.'"

CHAPTER VI.

RESULTS.

TWENTY-FIVE years of toil have also been years of triumph for Christ's cause. While, as in all other modes of good-doing, much of the labor may *seem* lost, there are yet actual and unquestioned results, which swell away beyond our limits of record. The variety also of these results is such as to increase the difficulty of presenting them in a condensed form. Yet illustrations will be given, under various heads, enough, at least, to convey a hint of the work and its reward.

Forestalling bad by good books. When this can be done a vantage-ground is gained of untold value to the prevalence of truth. Vice, like noxious weeds, having obtained the ground, is hard to eradicate. First fill the measure with wheat, and there is no room for chaff. Nor should it be overlooked that books, good or bad, have a tenfold influence in new countries, where the people are scattered, with little to occupy their minds in intellectual, or even in social channels. On Sabbath days, and days of storm and rain, and during periods of sickness, many long hours are unemployed, and the active mind of the frontiersman seeks occupation. Place in his hand a book, and it is not thrown aside at a glance to be forgotten; but in many cases is read, and reread, and thought over, and discussed, and then reëxamined, until it becomes a part of his mental and moral being. Hence the power of books in colporteur fields. If vile literature, in the form of trashy novels, infidel books, or licentious pamphlets, is diffused by the craft of the devil in a forming community in advance of a saving literature, most disastrous are the fruits, and long years of Christian effort are necessary to supplant these and instal the writers whose words are life. And here colportage may come with its swift foot, and ready tongue, and beneficent hand, to preoccupy the ground, and guard the scattered dwellers against the coming flood of desolating issues from the obscene and infidel press. Indeed, colporteurs' reports are crowded with instances, in which, as in the apostles' day, bad books "were brought together and burned" to give place to the truth.

"I sold 'Nelson's Cause and Cure' to an infidel. He afterwards told me that when he bought it, his tables and shelves were filled with novels. 'When I read Nelson, I gathered them up, took off the griddle from the stove, and shoved them in.' He is now a preacher of the gospel."

Another says: "On my first visit, many inquired for novels, and books on Universalism and infidelity, and many had them. On my second call, I was told that many of the bad books had been burned. The parents were very anxious to keep out the vicious reading, having seen its ruinous effects."

"In a great many instances I have had the pleasure of seeing the most profane works burned, and Bunyan, Baxter, and Doddridge, received in their stead. At a sale, one day, I noticed Paine's 'Age of Reason;' but when offered by the auctioneer, the old lady said that was her husband's favorite book, and it must not be sold out of the family. I went next day and offered her the Bible and Baxter for it, which she accepted. She and her children became pious, and often thanked God that the American Tract Society had sent me there; for, said she, 'If you had not brought me those precious books, I should have held on to Paine, and died as the old man did.'" Another says, "I have frequently exchanged my books for bad ones, and have put this corrupt and worthless stuff where it could never be read again."

But the effect of circulating standard evangelical books by the thousand, and the hundred thousand, in the waste places of our country, vastly transcends in importance the mere destruction of a few volumes of the vile. They become a permanent power for good, laying the foundation of character in thousands of households, where the corrupting literature will no longer be tolerated. "The desire for religious reading has been greatly increased on my field," writes a faithful worker; "and parents will no longer permit their children to read the miserable stuff heretofore so common." "By the twenty-four thousand volumes I have circulated," writes another, "great good has already resulted. Vicious literature has been counteracted, novel readers have given up their trash, and some have embraced the Saviour." "In creating a taste for good reading and counteracting the bad," says one, "no tongue can tell the influence of the seventeen thousand five hundred volumes of truth I have circulated in the last seven years. I see the results constantly." "When I commenced my work, religious books were rare and novels abundant," writes another; "now, tables that formerly groaned under the load of soul-destroying literature are filled with the issues of the Tract and other good societies." Here then, in preoccupying the ground, or in driving out the vile and installing the good, colportage has reaped some of its most precious rewards.

Colportage promotes the Sabbath-school cause. True, it is not specifically a Sabbath-school enterprise, neither is it primarily a Bible distributor; and yet it labors largely in both directions. A true Bible Christian, such as every colporteur should be, cannot leave any family unsupplied with the precious Source of all his hope, and the American Bible Society nobly responds to his request for the power to supply each destitute family he may find. An earnest lover of children, as every true colporteur is, cannot leave any neighborhood destitute of a Sabbath-school where one can be formed, and his thorough visiting of every house reveals the number of children ungathered; while his stores of children's books enable him to fit them out with a suitable library. Hence a large and blessed incidental result of this system is its aid to the Sabbath-school cause.

Especially in the newer districts, every colporteur accomplishes something in this line. One describes a county canvassed, containing fifteen thousand children, of whom less than three thousand attended Sabbath-school. He formed twelve new schools for these destitute ones, supplying them with the beginning of a library, and enlisted good people in the work of teaching. Another, referring to a former year's work in a Southern state, notes, "In that year I organized nine schools, embracing four hundred scholars. One of these stood the shock of war, being in the very midst of it. They have procured preaching, and enjoyed a precious revival of religion, the fruits of which the various evangelical denominations are realizing." Another, who has travelled above twenty thousand miles on foot and on horseback, and visited fourteen thousand four hundred families during the seven years of his service, says, "I have been instrumental in forming eighteen schools, and supplying many others with books." One laborer, who has been in the service for eighteen years, in giving an interesting account of his work, adds, "I have aided in forming one hundred and thirty-five schools in these years." Who can estimate the value for time and eternity of such a service?

A still larger work is reported by a godly man, who has long toiled on in a mountainous and neglected district--neglected until he went there, now supplied very generally with the preached gospel: "I have organized one hundred and seventy-eight Sabbath-schools, where there had never been any before. In some of these places the people were so poor they could not purchase even the tickets to commence with, and I have taken in pay for books, Irish potatoes, maple sugar, and other produce, and hauled it thirty-five miles to market. After a time, they began to save money to buy books. One youth offered to buy a large Testament if I would take a gallon of brandy he had just brought from the still-house, and promised he would never drink another drop. I closed the bargain, took the jug, and broke it over a rock. He has since become a Christian, and is doing well in a worldly point of view."

Such facts, running through the entire history of the enterprise, demonstrate the value of Union Missionary Colportage to the youth of our land, and these are but isolated specimens. A superintendent over one agency has left a record of above seven hundred Sabbath-schools formed on his field by colporteurs. Some of the results, in numerous conversions and the formation of churches, will appear in the following pages; the entire results in the great day.

Colportage aiding the Ministry. Colportage is designed to be helpful to the ministry of every true church of Christ. Its rules of action, its specific instructions to every worker, its means of influence, all intend the furtherance of truth and righteousness; and the committee who have it in charge rejoice to know, from evidence constant and accumulating, that it meets an almost universal approval from ministers and people over our entire land. Those who prefer to work in strictly denominational channels, still endorse it as adapted to the "regions beyond," while most rejoice in its hearty and efficient coöperation in every good word and work, and more especially in periods of gracious reviving. And the value of its aid directly to the faithful and overworked minister is gratefully acknowledged in thousands of instances.

Says one, writing the Society, "Your literature has contributed largely to the extension of Christ's kingdom among us, by breaking up the fallow ground of the heart, and preparing it to receive the word preached." Another writes to the colporteur, "I thank you for your labors among inquirers and the young converts during our precious revival. God has abundantly blessed your work. I feel that our church and myself owe a deep debt of obligation to you and your Society." Another, "I have been quickened to more activity by the perusal of the soul-stirring publications. The 'Reformed Pastor' I prize greatly, and while perusing it, have been instructed and stirred up, and I hope to become a better minister of Jesus Christ."

In addition to the direct aid afforded the minister, the colporteur not unfrequently awakes among his people the determination to supply his library, often too meagre for his needs, with valuable additions from the standard works of the Society, thus the better equipping him for his laborious work. And in many ways, as a fellow-helper, the colporteur passes from church to church sowing good seed, which the ministry harvest for God. This is recorded among the results of colportage in a vast number of cases.

Conversions and Revivals. While looking at these evidences of God's mercy in saving sinners, we would be far from claiming colportage as the single, or in many cases the principal instrument. The agencies for conversion which the Holy Spirit uses are manifold, and often, in their operation, inscrutable to human vision; and the most unseen are sometimes the most efficient. The hearing of a single sermon, the reading of a single tract, a chance remark by a stranger, a prayer offered in the family, even a blessing asked at a meal, may be the immediate instrument, in God's hand, of arresting the attention and riveting conviction, leading to the surrender of the soul to Christ. Yet the preparation for this may have been long years of faithful preaching, and the prayers and instructions of pious and now sainted parents. All this we do not forget in the incidents which follow. True, there are many cases where colportage, to human view, was almost the sole instrument; yet even here we would refer all to infinite mercy, and praise God that he can use the feeblest instrumentality in snatching men from destruction. But it is right, in sketching the history of this mode of Christian effort, to note, for the strengthening of our faith, how richly the divine blessing seems to attend it. Instances might be multiplied by hundreds.

Let the first illustrate as well the power as the grace of God, in rescuing a family from the deepest degradation, and lifting its members to the dignity of fellow-heirs to an eternal inheritance. "Far in the mountains I entered a cabin, without windows or floor, and found a family of ten children, not one of whom could read a word, nor had they ever heard a sermon. The father was unable to read, and was dreadfully profane, uttering an oath in every sentence, even when speaking of serious things. The mother could read imperfectly, but was very ignorant. I held a long conversation with the old man, who claimed to be an infidel because his employer boasted of being one, though this poor man did not know what the word meant. He admitted a belief in a future state of awards, and with an oath declared he was not fit for a holy world. After he left the house, the mother showed deep anxiety on the subject of religion, and begged me *to leave it for her, so she might get it.* She had some time heard talk of 'getting religion.' The husband refused to accept a Bible, saying, 'the old woman would spend all her time trying to read it;' and she was unwilling to take it, after he left, lest he should find it and abuse her.

However, I determined to put the Bible where she could 'get it,' and so placed it under the steps as I left the house. I subsequently learned the result. This cabin was six miles from the settlement, and the old man was often away all day, and she had time to spell out much of the New Testament. She read to the children, three of whom were grown girls, and they became interested. At length she felt that she must pray, and exacting a promise from the children that they would not tell the father, she commenced to pray with them. One evening the old man came in unexpectedly, and found her reading the Bible. 'Oh, ho, how is this? Just as I expected; that fellow that prayed here left it, did he? *Well, old woman, read some for us.*' She commenced, and read slowly of Christ being led out to Calvary and nailed to the cross, and that two thieves were nailed, one on each side of him. He stopped her, and with an oath told her to read it again, and again. At length he retired. She found the light dawning on her mind, and was able to accept of Christ as her Saviour; and in the fullness of her heart, felt she must pray with her children, and commit them to her new-found Saviour. But the old man, though quiet, was not asleep; and her prayers and rejoicings, 'I've got religion, I've got religion, bless the Lord,' reached his heart. In the morning he went out to the woods, and tried to pray; and when he returned, he called his wife, and said, 'Mother, gather the family; I swear I must be a Christian;' and with a great oath, which he did not mean to be profane, he promised to be the Lord's, and from that hour commenced his service. Of all this I knew nothing; but in my travels I determined to call again upon the family. I went at the middle of the day, when I supposed the old man would be away. To my astonishment, I saw him before I reached the house, and checked my horse, for I was afraid of him. He ran out with his arms expanded, crying, 'Bless God for sending you here again,' and pulled me off my horse, and actually carried me in his arms into the house. He told me the whole story of his conversion, and I could not doubt its reality. He was a new man. I sent them a preacher, who instructed them more fully in the truth, and *the parents and nine of the children professed faith in Christ.*" Such is a specimen of the direct result of colportage.

Known to the writer are the following facts, as connected with a single colporteur's labors, and he a humble, modest man. An impenitent, but educated youth became convinced, from closely watching his conduct, that religion was a reality, and after a time of inquiry, was brought to Christ through his instrumentality. He first became a voluntary colporteur, visiting the poor and wicked families around, and praying with them; then he studied theology, all the while working successfully for the Lord; at length he went a missionary to India, and for years taught the heathen the way of life; failing in health, he returned, and is now a most zealous and effective minister of Christ. This colporteur visited another student in college; was at first repulsed, but continued his efforts, and the student became eminently pious, and went to Africa to preach for the Saviour. After a faithful service, and recently, he has gone home. Perhaps a score of men have been called into the ministry, more or less directly through this man's agency, and his four sons are in the sacred office, while numerous conversions have occurred all along his history of twenty years in this work.

"In going over my former field last summer," reports a godly brother, "I found about twenty, with whom, when impenitent, I had conversed and prayed, who now were rejoicing in hope. One young lady, in whose school I had pleaded with the children to give their hearts to Christ, was herself convicted, and I was present the next summer when she made a profession of religion. She told me that her salvation was owing to God's blessing upon the talk to her school."

Another writes, "In this place, there followed my distributions a great interest, and many were brought to repentance; and the work so increased that I devoted my time to the inquirers, and others sold my books, and the result was a large increase in the churches around." Another: "About four hundred have been added to the different churches on my field, not that my labors and books were the only, or the principal cause, yet I am sure the good seed sown for years has at length taken root downward, and borne fruit upward." A faithful brother in Missouri enumerates in detail nine hopeful conversions directly through the agency of the colporteur's visits and books. "The pastor told me," says another, "that of the forty accessions to his church immediately following my labors there, a number were awakened by the books and tracts." A brother who has labored thirteen years, circulated thirty-three thousand volumes, travelled above fifty-eight thousand miles, and made more than nineteen thousand family visits, after speaking of many cases of conversion, gives this incident: "I called upon a family whose head was skeptical, but courteous. The Lord seemed to help me in conversation, and his heart was touched. He bought Watson's 'Reply to Paine.' In a short time he embraced Christ. I met him a few years after, when he told me he considered my first visit to his house the starting point not only of his own, but his wife's and two daughters' religious life." But why should instances be here multiplied, when the entire history of the work is illuminated by such cases?

Result in founding Churches. If Union Missionary Colportage is thus blessed to the conversion of many souls, we should naturrally look for the springing up of churches in its wake. Such has been the fact in very many cases, especially in the newer settlements. God is using this system as a forerunning agency to the organization of local and permanent worshipping assemblies.

"I labored awhile," reports a clerical colporteur, "in a neighborhood where Sabbath breaking, profanity, and all sin, abounded; but could sell no books. I made an appointment to preach in a school-house, and there was a good attendance. The love of God and the story of the cross, melted their hearts. I had to continue the meetings for three weeks. A church was formed, a house of worship built, and a general reformation wrought. A good many Universalists gave up their errors, and are useful members of the church."

A brother who had labored on one field for ten years, and had sold twenty thousand volumes, given away six thousand, and travelled on foot, horseback, and in a buggy, above twelve thousand weary, toilsome miles, writes, "Sabbath-schools and churches have been originated all over my field since I commenced, and many of them attribute their origin and prosperity largely to the colporteur work." An earnest brother, in a mountainous region, avers: "Over much of my wide field, preachers have followed my labors, and organized considerable congregations. Take one district as an example. In the whole region of B—— there was no preaching when I commenced. After laboring about twelve months among the people, I succeeded in obtaining a godly United Brethren's minister, who went with me into the mountains, and for seven weeks we held most precious meetings. As a consequence, at the next conference they laid out a circuit on that territory, and every preaching-place was at a point where I had organized a Sabbath-school. That circuit has now three ministers."

In training Workers for Christ. Work for Christ has a fourfold reward: in the approval of God, in the good done, in the happiness of the worker, and *in his increased power of usefulness for the future.* The development of muscular, and brain, and heart power, depends upon exercise, and he who employs them all in active exertion for Christ will grow to be a symmetrical and stalwart Christian. Only by vigorous and long-continued exercise, and in great variety of circumstances, does any one attain to that ideal of Christian character presented by the apostle, in which, to faith is added manly courage, scriptural knowledge, personal control, untiring patience, great devoutness, brotherly kindness, and an enlarged catholicity. 2 Peter 1: 5–7. How beautifully colportage, by its union principles, Christian aims, and infinite variety of opportunities for exercise, works to this end, could be illustrated to an indefinite extent.

The constant trials to which the faithful laborer is subjected, strengthen his graces and develop his powers for greater contests and victories. A plain, uneducated man grows even eloquent in describing his experience: "Has any been sneered at as a canting hypocrite? so have I. Has any been jeered as getting his living without work? so have I. Has any been ordered home to attend to his own business, and let others' alone? so have I. Has any been driven violently out of the house? so have I. Has any been threatened with mob violence? so have I. Has any been refused Christian hospitality? so have I, many a time. But none of these things move me, and I can humbly say, 'I count not my life dear unto me, if I may win souls to my Saviour.' Has any received, day by day, the witness of the Spirit; has any found kind friends day by day; found grace in every time of need; had a foretaste of the joy in reserve for the righteous; and been strengthened with might in the inner man for every good word and work? I more; for God is with me."

Another describes and rejoices in this work, so admirable for developing the Christian graces: "None but self-denying followers of the Redeemer can hope for success. I remember the first day I went out to labor: not meeting with immediate success, I wept bitterly; but before the day's work was finished I was rejoicing. It will not do for the colporteur, when he comes to a house, to halt and shout, 'Hallo,' and from the roadside inquire if there is any thing in the way of religious books wanted. No; he must dismount, tie up, and enter the house, and with a confiding love in his Redeemer unknown to many professed Christians, beseech and entreat the inmates, whom he never expects to see again, not only to take his books, but to be reconciled to God. It is not the rich that take him by the hand generally; but the poor in this world's goods, and the lowly that oftenest cheer his heart. Although I have met with many kind-hearted people of wealth, still they are the exceptions. And if ever the American Tract Society shines with a sweet and heavenly lustre, it is in this very thing, that it bears the gospel to the poor, and seals the word by pointing the inquiring, the erring, and the hardened sinner to Jesus. If all the admonitions, encouragings, warnings, entreaties, expostulations, prayers, wrestlings, cryings, heart-breakings, hungerings, thirstings, wettings and scorchings by the way, insults of sinners, and greetings of friends, dialogues and arguments made use of and endured by the colporteur in his labors for a series of years, were accurately set down and penned in a book, the result would be overwhelming; yet, blessed be God, though my trials are not known to man, they are known above, and the humble servant who has not shrunk from duty in the hour of severest trial will receive a gracious crown in the day when He comes to make up His jewels. I look upon my work as matchless in grandeur."

A little German errand boy is trained up to the ministry of the glorious gospel by colportage: "In the year 1853 I was employed in St. Louis as errand boy for the depository. After a time, I became clerk. While in the depository, by reading such works as 'Baxter's Call,' 'Come to Jesus,' and the Memoirs of Martyn and Brainerd, I was enabled to consecrate myself to Christ, and experience his pardoning mercy. The reading of 'Harlan Page,' 'Claudius Buchanan,' and James' 'Christian Progress,' awakened in me a desire to do good. My first efforts consisted in the distribution of tracts in destitute portions of the city. In connection with three other young men, I took part in the organization of a mission Sabbath-school, and for three years filled the position of treasurer in it. The school now has an average attendance of fourteen hundred. In 1857 another person and myself established another mission Sabbath-school in the northwestern part of the city. The majority of the scholars were secured by our personal solicitation while engaged in tract visitation. During my connection with both schools, a number of conversions blessed the labors of the teachers. During the revival season in 1857, the cheaper publications of the Society were extensively used. Four persons attributed their salvation to the tract, 'The Act of Faith.' One was savingly blessed by reading, 'Behold the Lamb of God.' 'A Pastor's Counsel' was put into the hands of every young convert, and with the happiest results. The spirit which made the lives of Henry Martyn and Edward Payson fragrant with self-sacrificing labors, impelled me to make a fuller consecration of myself to Christ, and to endeavor from the pulpit to point the perishing to the atoning Saviour on the cross." He is now proclaiming the good news.

We add another example of one trained by colportage for wide usefulness, until this hour devoting himself with increasing strength to its prosecution: "Some time in the year 1839, being then at my father's house in South Carolina, in my fifteenth year, and nearly deaf and dumb, secluded from the world, in the midst of deep and impenetrable swamps, surrounded by about six thousand five hundred negroes, and hardly twenty-five whites in all, and these ignorant and tyrannical overseers, a colporteur of the American Tract Society visited father, soliciting the sale of the Evangelical Family Library of fifteen volumes. When father was about to decline, I induced him to purchase them for me. I commenced reading the first volume, Doddridge's 'Rise and Progress,' was soon convicted and converted by God's grace. The last volume, 'Life of J. B. Taylor,' convicted father. I immediately commenced reading every night to the negroes, until I read nearly all of the volumes to them, and many were converted. I joined the church, and was appointed class-leader, and commenced visiting from house to house, reading and circulating books and tracts as fast as I was able to buy or beg them. I also commenced Sabbath-schools for the blacks, but was often molested, until at length I was appointed captain of the patrol, which gave me access to these people. I at length obtained license to exhort and travel on a circuit; but gave my whole attention to the circulation of books, getting them from pastors and elsewhere, until 1853, when the preachers at Raleigh, who had witnessed my work, and Bishop Early said, 'God has called M—— to the book business.' I was then introduced to Mr. C——, who soon got me a commission from the Tract Society; and I have worked ever since. My entire work may be summed up thus: Sales and grants, $12,000; miles travelled, seventy thousand; family visits, fifty-three thousand. I have travelled on foot over thirty thousand miles, and yet I am to-day in good health, and can stand fatigue as well as ever I could. I have worked in six different states. On receiving my commission, I went before God in prayer for aid and direction. On surveying my field I found an almost total destitution of religious books and piety, and the people served by many illiterate preachers. Their religion was either very cold and formal, or of the extreme spasmodic kind, all feeling without knowledge. I saw clearly that the tract volumes stood a happy medium between these two extremes, quickening the one to zeal and heartfelt religion, while it tamed the wild animal excitement of the other. Nothing has ever done for my own church more than the tract volumes. To use an elder's language, 'Brother, your books build up our church more than all the big, shouting revivals, because they quietly instruct, and lasting impressions are made. There is a holy spirit which pervades every page; no one can read even a few pages without being moistened to tears.' In this way they forestall vicious books. God does bless the book, even if the devil should carry it, to the salvation of souls. A stolen one has, to my knowledge, converted the thief. I have organized one hundred and seventy-six Sabbath and day schools of nearly five thousand eight hundred scholars; one of one hundred and forty in 1855, which is still in operation. I have always aided pastors and churches in every possible way; in visiting every house, distributing tracts, and begging the people to attend church; and praying with the people in their houses, fields, shops, on the roadside, and everywhere I can find them, and instructing their children and servants. I have always sought out the lowly ones, and cheered them."

What a record of development and Christian effort, for one who at the age of fifteen was an ignorant boy, almost deaf and dumb, in secluded rice swamps, and with no means of education!

CHAPTER VII.

A COMPREHENSIVE VIEW.

But an imperfect idea of the toil, self-denial, true apostolic labor, and large success of colportage can be obtained by the selection of isolated incidents, as in the preceding chapter. A condensed view of the work of years may aid the mind in comprehending the value of the system to the cause of Christ.

An Individual Record. "I have travelled on foot, horseback, and in buggy, in nine years, thirty-five thousand miles; have made fifty-eight thousand family visits; have circulated twenty-four thousand seven hundred volumes; have assisted in organizing fourteen Sabbath-schools, and have seen six churches springing up on my field, in more or less intimate connection with my labors." Brief is this record of solitary journeyings, which in the aggregate would girdle the globe, of the Christian visits to many thousand households, of the number of volumes of saving truth installed in destitute families, and of Sabbath-schools and churches formed; but no one can doubt the vast reach of these two thousand seven hundred days of personal service for the Master. And this is but one of many similar records on the files of the Society.

A Partial View. In the following table we group a few statistics from a small number of laborers, bringing out the magnitude of the work in three aspects.

Initials of Laborers.	Length of Service.	Volumes Circulated.	Family Visits made.	Miles Travelled.
J. W. W.----	2 y'rs.	6,400	9,100	2,500
J. McR.-----	2 "	8,000	5,500	5,200
J. M.-------	3 "	9,000	6,200	6,700
J. M.-------	7 "	26,000	19,000	15,500
J. P.--------	7 "	18,200	14,400	20,500
J. M.-------	7 "	24,000	11,600	12,000
G. S.-------	8 "	35,000	25,500	51,000
H. S.-------	8 "	18,900	20,700	24,000
G. W. S.----	8½ "	19,900	21,700	24,200
G. T. H.----	9½ "	27,700	58,400	35,000
B. J.-------	10 "	35,200	24,900	15,000
J. D.--------	10½ "	30,100	28,200	7,500
T. C.-------	10½ "	29,900	18,400	21,000
P. B.-------	11 "	20,500	26,500	16,600
A. O. C.-----	13 "	34,000	44,500	12,000
D. D. S.-----	13 "	33,100	18,900	58,200
	130 "	375,900	353,500	326,900

This table shows as the average that each colporteur, in each year of colportage, circulated two thousand eight hundred and ninety-one volumes, made two thousand seven hundred and nineteen family Christian visits, and traversed two thousand five hundred and fourteen miles from house to house. Add to this the social meetings addressed, the words of exhortation and comfort spoken, the Sabbath-schools formed, and the unnumbered influences flowing from such labor, and we may form some idea of the efficiency of the system. Even this partial table is worthy of study.

General Summary of Statistics. So far as mere statistics can exhibit the results of a missionary work, we are happily in possession of the most accurate data. During the quarter of a century that colportage has been expanding, the laborers have systematically reported monthly, quarterly, and annually, and in duplicate. These reports are on file, and afford the means of comparison and correction in each case. The following summary is therefore full upon the points it touches, and as accurate as care can make it; while, of course, it only attempts to give certain great facts wrought out by the system.

SUMMARY VIEW OF COLPORTAGE FOR TWENTY-FIVE YEARS.

Time employed, months	48,499
Number of volumes sold	8,233,620
" " granted	2,264,356
" public meetings addressed, and prayer-meetings held	222,015
" families destitute of all religious books except the Bible	793,743
" families destitute of the Bible	489,013
" families of Roman-catholics	817,637
" families habitually neglecting evangelical preaching	1,261,285
" families conversed with on personal religion, or prayed with	4,874,256
" family visits	9,354,485

When we say, in summing up the work, that above four thousand years of colporteur labor have been performed, more than the continuous service of two men from the birth of Christ until now; that ten and a half millions of volumes of saving truth have been circulated; that more than two hundred thousand religious meetings have been addressed; that nearly a million of families have been found destitute of religious books, and supplied; that a million and a quarter of families have been found who neglected evangelical worship, and have been urged to duty; that the gospel has been carried to nearly one million Roman-catholic families; and that of the more than nine million Christian visits made to families, five millions of them were accompanied with prayer or direct personal appeals in the name of Christ—we have given figures which, in their influence for the glory of God, sweep far beyond our feeble comprehension. This general summary of facts we present for examination and reflection. An eloquent speaker at one of the anniversaries exclaimed, "Why these are like the figures of astronomy; they make us think of the leaves of our forests, or the countless waves that gleam along our extended coast!"

Of the *full* results of these labors we shall not be informed until the enlarged capacities of the eternal world shall qualify us to comprehend the realities which will be there revealed. But when one of the many hundreds of colporteurs that have been employed tells us of over *seven hundred Sabbath-schools* organized in connection with his labors; and another tells us of one hundred and three conversions coming to his personal knowledge as resulting from the circulation of copies of one tract by him; and another tells us of three churches growing out of the labors of one colporteur in a single district; and others continually report to us in their correspondence individual cases of conversion, and interesting revivals of religion more or less directly connected with their labors; when watchmen from the walls of Zion report to us their own conversion by the reading of some of these publications; "a mission established among the heathen as the result of the reading of one tract published by this Society;" a revival of religion, resulting in the conversion of several hundreds of souls, from the systematic circulation of the Tract Society's volumes, accompanied with fireside labors from house to house; and when we find the record of such statements as these running through the whole history of the Society, and constantly meet with similar facts everywhere in our intercourse with Christian men—we are constrained to exclaim, "What hath God wrought!" and to accept the conviction that truly our labors have not been in vain, while from the heart we exclaim, "Not unto us, O Lord, not unto us, but unto thy name give the glory."

CONCLUSION.

In the foregoing pages we have described the system of Union Missionary Colportage, as originated and conducted by the American Tract Society; have attempted to point out its true place, as a forerunner to the organized churches, antagonistic to none, helpful to all; have illustrated the need of such an agency, from the divided state of the church of Christ, and the fearful destitutions which exist over large portions of our land; have indicated the happy adaptation of this Union agency to the peculiar exigencies of our country; and have shown by a series of illustrations the versatility of the system to relieve every spiritual want and woe of our scattered and perishing population.

Further, we have presented some of the results of twenty-five years of colportage, in forestalling bad by good books, in promoting Sabbath-schools, in aiding the ministry, in conversions and revivals, and in founding churches; and have shown the power of the system in training active and stalwart Christians for the work of the Lord; and finally, we have summed up, as far as figures could do this, a few of the unnumbered results achieved during the first quarter century of Union Missionary Colportage.

From all of which there seem to us to follow irresistibly these four conclusions:

That there has existed, and continues to exist, an imperative need of Union Missionary Colportage over much of our land;

That there is a special field for such a system as is prosecuted by this Society;

That in the present divided state of the evangelical churches, its catholicity adapts it to perform a grand evangelizing work, in which good men of all names can coöperate;

And that the results, thus far, give the highest sanction to a speedy enlargement, and the most earnest prosecution of the system in the future.

So far as this volume shall cheer and aid our brethren whose toil it attempts to portray; so far as it shall incline pastors to commend the enterprise to the prayers and benefactions of their people; so far as it shall suggest to benevolent men of means the blessed privilege of proclaiming Christ to thousands by sustaining a colporteur in a destitute section; so far as it shall stimulate private Christians to faith, and prayer, and personal effort unceasingly for the salvation of sinners—thus far will it have accomplished the end of its preparation. We commit it to that gracious God who can bless the feeblest instrumentality, and to the dear brethren of every name who love our Lord Jesus Christ, and look for his coming and kingdom.

APPENDIX.

To illustrate many points briefly presented in the preceding pages, the statements of men who have labored in the various departments of the work will be found valuable.

STATEMENTS OF COLPORTEURS.

A clerical colporteur, who speaks and writes in both German and English, though imperfectly in the latter, thus graphically describes his work:

I have labored the last fifteen years and forty days as a colporteur. I have sold about $6,200, and granted $900; travelled about sixty-five thousand seven hundred miles. I made fifty-four thousand three hundred family visits, and labored for ten thousand soldiers. The influence from $7,100 worth of our Christian books, which I have brought to families in my field, is very great. There is little inquiry for novels any more; I hear the question, perhaps only once a month, if I have novels among my books. Many Christians, through my influence, are talking against novels and other wicked books. When I started, fifteen years ago, there was inquiry for novels, perhaps more or less every day; but now they want our Christian books, and there is taste for Christian reading nearly everywhere. True Christian religion has made great progress here, through our Christian literature. I have helped in organizing Sabbath-schools, brought in teachers and scholars, given addresses, and introduced much of our Christian literature. My whole soul is engaged for their increase and prospering.

I visited, some time ago, a German Roman-catholic family with many children; I spoke to the parents about sending their children to the Sabbath-school, and gave them cards, but the children appeared very ignorant about my questions in religion; they could not read. But before a year was past I came again in that settlement; the children received me very happy, and began to read English in my books. Full of joy, I inquired, "Where did you learn to read so well?" They said, "Have you not told us, when you were here, we shall go to the Sabbath-school? We did go, and learned it in our Sabbath-school." Soon that family moved away in a Yankee settlement, and my heart was full of praise, because I believe they are lost to the pope for ever, and they find Jesus. I gave them some of our Christian literature, told them they shall read the Bible and give their hearts to Jesus.

I spoke with another family about religion, sending their children to common-school and Sabbath-school, sold them books, and directed that German family to Jesus; also they went to Sabbath-school and English meeting. Last year was a great revival of religion in that settlement, and father, and mother, and four children became converted, and joined the church. Close by, there is another Roman-catholic man; his wife is Protestant. I spoke with that man much about religion, left them many tracts and books; his wife also became converted in the same revival, joined the church, and the children are in Sabbath-schools. The man was under conviction, but did not find Jesus. His wife has family worship every day now. That man is also out of popery, and his whole family; I hope they all found Jesus.

In another settlement I held meetings sometimes among Roman-catholics and Protestants; brought them many tracts, good books, and Bibles. After that there was revival of religion, and a number of them became converted. Some are leading men now in the Christian church. I am acquainted with many who have been brought up in popish darkness, not much better than heathen; now they are happy Christians. God is sending us many thousands of heathen right before our door. God and the angels are looking down from heaven to see what we do for their souls. Shall they be neglected right before our doors? Are unconverted souls before our doors not so much worth as souls in India, Africa, or China? And be sure if Christians do n't do their duty to their unconverted neighbors around them, they will suffer for it in the future. Perhaps they fight against our Sundays, or for popery, and will lead our children with them to hell. God help us, that we do our duty towards them. I am a great friend of missions among heathen, and my prayer has been since I was twelve years old, "Lord, make me a missionary, and send me to the heathen." God has heard my prayer. Christians, lead souls to Christ, so many as you can, in foreign countries, but do n't neglect unconverted souls in our own country. God sometimes saves souls through the reading of a tract.

I have labored a great deal in revivals. Ministers are inviting me to come and labor with them. I have started meetings; preached sometimes two or three weeks every night, and on Sundays two, sometimes three times; and through the day I labored from house to house as a colporteur. And glory be to God in the highest, he has saved and converted many souls. I work for revival the whole year. Thank God, great revivals are right before us. The Spirit of the Lord is working now in many places. I work with the Spirit of the Lord, and stir Christians up, and tell them they shall lead sinners to Christ. But we need colportage work everywhere. There is not a whole town or settlement in my field yet where every soul is converted. Yes, not one-half from the whole population is yet converted. We need colportage labor everywhere through the whole land, till Christ comes the second time.

May nobody tell me about stopping colporteur labor! I shall, with the help of God, never stop. No, never. And when my body is lying in the grave shall my soul pray before God's throne, "Lord, save souls."

I thought perhaps I labor too hard in the Lord's vineyard, and come before it is time in the grave; but thank God, he is saving souls, and I am willing to go home when the Lord calls me. One time I thought heaven is very near to me; Oh, I wish I could go home to glory just now; but in a little while I thought God's Spirit is telling me, We can get along very well without you in heaven; but remember, your time has not come yet; we need you yet in Illinois. You can do more for the Lord's cause there yet than you can do at home in glory. By-and-by you shall come home, and rest from your labor; but for the present we want you to work more for Jesus in Illinois. Amen, said I, blessed Jesus; I am not my own; do as thou pleasest; work through whom thou pleasest; but Oh, my Saviour, save many precious souls for thy own name's sake. Amen.

Now let me take my basket with soul-saving literature, let me stand surrounded on one side by Jesus and those that became converted through the Tract Society, and on the other side by Roman-catholics, drunkards, swearers, Sabbath-breakers, and others. Now inquire, shall we stop colporteur work? The wicked will halloo, Yes; but Christians will shout through the air, and angels would shout down here and in glory, No, never, *never*, NEVER.

J. C. D.

While men of such fiery zeal and tireless perseverance as above presented can be found, colportage will never lack friends, nor be without God's blessing.

Hard Work and its Fruits. A fearless pioneer, who, for eleven years, has toiled in the mountains of East Tennessee, the swamps of Arkansas and southeastern Missouri, the wilds of Iowa, and the plains of Kansas, shrinking from no toil and avoiding no self-denial, gives an impressive account "of streams swam, mountains climbed, caves penetrated, swamps threaded, and exposures endured; but the lost were found, the weak strengthened, the dying comforted, and the preparatory work done, resulting in the organization of several churches. In one portion of my field one-half the families were destitute of Bibles, and all religious books, with but few schools, and fewer churches. Yet here I sold and gave several hundred dollars' worth of books, organized Sabbath-schools wherever I could find one suitable person to take charge of each, and employed four other colporteurs who prosecuted the work in the swamps, until sickness or death closed their labors. But the good seed brought forth a rich harvest. Two years after my labors there, I learned from one of my fellow-laborers that a church had sprung from nearly every Sabbath-school formed, and a presbytery had grown mainly out of this forerunning work. Another colporteur told me he had organized several churches since closing his labors, and that a new impetus had been given to religion and a new cast to society through this agency." D. M. S.

How feeble a conception does such a recital as above, give of the days of toil and nights of sleeplessness, the exposure to sun, and rain, and malaria, to coarse food and the coarser conduct of the people; to insult and abuse, and the heartlessness of even some professed Christians, which were endured in order to reach these neglected thousands. Colportage is no holiday sport, but stern, hard work. The incarnate Saviour trod no pathway of flowers, nor should his followers desire an easier lot.

A Day's Work and its Results, as narrated by a colporteur, who for thirteen years and three months has faithfully toiled, travelling nineteen thousand miles, often on foot, visiting seventeen thousand families, and circulating $5,300 worth of good books, demand a record. It was a winter day, the snow deep, and the wind bitterly cold. His first call was cheerless, a young man scorning his exhortations and sneering at religion while he prayed with the family. His next visit was to a husband and wife backslidden from religion, but tearful when he left. Seven more families were visited, and not one person found who loved the Saviour. As night drew on and the cold increased, he could find no place of rest and entertainment, being repeatedly refused. At length, in deep darkness and almost exhausted, he found a home and a Christian welcome; but dispirited and wayworn, and tempted to give up so hard a work. In after-years, a subsequent visit revealed these facts: the backsliders were reclaimed, and walking in Christ, the sneering youth had become a preacher, a revival had followed, a church was organized in the neighborhood, and he was assured that the starting-point of it all was that wintry day's work. God be praised that he can use so feeble instrumentality in so great a work. T. P. R.

The Power of the Press among the Destitute is well illustrated by the letter of a brother who labored as colporteur for eighteen years in Central Virginia, until the war. He describes the state of society when he commenced, the paucity of good books, the masses of ignorant people, the prevalence of crime, the want of Sabbath-schools, and the inability of the ministry to reach even half the people with sacred instruction; and then shows how faithful and toilsome labor from house to house, year after year, in many places brought almost the entire population under gospel influences, aided the churches, multiplied Sabbath-schools, and put a new face on society. He closes with the words, "I am fully convinced that there is a power in the system of union colportage coöperating with the churches of Christ which is *indispensable* for the speedy evangelization of the destitute millions.

"We have a special duty in regard to the press used now so extensively for evil. Its power for good is unlimited, especially among those beyond the reach of the living ministry, who with ability to read, are yet starving for mental food." C. A. R.

The permeating and attracting power of union colportage is well presented by one who has labored long in North Carolina. "A prudent colporteur," he declares, "can go into any and every family in his field. Wealth, intelligence, high position in society, commanding influence for good or evil, poverty, ignorance, vice, want, with all their train of sorrows and all their dark abodes of misery, alike claim and alike meet his visit; while, 'Lo I am with you alway,' encourages, directs, sustains, protects, prospers, blesses him. He acts as a moral *leveller* for society, softening down the self-sufficiency of the rich, and elevating the poor to a feeling of self-respect, a sense of duty and accountability to God. He comes to all as a friend. He sees their wants, and makes himself one of each family in plan, in effort, in encouragement to get good and do good. Whole families have followed me from house to house to see the books and to hear about Jesus; and in the long winter evenings three or four families would meet me at my lodging-place for reading, exhortation, and prayer. I once held a prayer-meeting by torchlight at a gold mine, the first ever known there; and for three days went from cabin to cabin, and shaft to shaft, talking, praying, and distributing tracts. In a year and a half thereafter a church of twenty-eight members was organized of these same miners."

After enumerating many instances of conversion, he adds, "Thus colportage diffuses knowledge among the ignorant, aids in learning to read, tells the simple truths of Christ, helps the people to comprehend the gospel, cherishes the movings of the Holy Spirit, aids in building up churches, and hastens the conversion of the world to God." J. N. A.

The advantages of the *union element* in this agency are strongly presented by a clerical colporteur, who has labored some years in a mountainous region of New England: "Is it not Christian charity? is it not obedience to the commands of Christ? is it not in accordance with the spirit and agencies of the gospel, to reach these destitutions with the common salvation, and urge men to flee from the wrath to come? This scheme, from the broad platform of evangelical truth and unstinted charity which it occupies, meets a hearty welcome. It builds no line fences. It does not assort the people, seeking for this or that sect. It exalts Christ, and seeks to win the soul and fit it for heaven. None regard it as sectarian but those who are intensely so themselves; none bring against it 'a railing accusation' except those who rail at all that is lovely and of good report. Such are the deep convictions which years of service among all classes of people have produced." A. L.

TESTIMONY OF EXPERIENCE.

A venerable father, who has labored eighteen years as agent, writes: The minds originating colportage must have been directed from heaven. It came into being in an important crisis in our national history, when our broad country was filling up with a rapidity unparalleled in the history of the world, and from all nations, trained under different forms of government, and of different religions, a heterogeneous mass, including much ignorance and error. The system in its development met an emergency, and supplied a great and pressing need. Even in portions of New York state over which I have annually passed, this need is seen. On either side of a mountain lying nearly parallel with the Hudson, rises a tier of churches, each covering six or eight miles square. Of the two to three hundred families nominally belonging to each church, not more than eighty to a hundred attend regularly; while in the mountain gorges there are many hundreds who never visit the sanctuary, living and dying without hope. These would have gone to the judgment unprepared, had you not sent a faithful colporteur to seek them out. Great good has followed his labors, and many souls have been converted. Similar instances have occurred in many parts of my field.

An intelligent and candid Romanist remarked to me, "You Protestants make no headway by preaching and writing against our system; but your colporteurs, warm-hearted and zealous, coming into our families, talking with parents and children, praying for each, and leaving books and tracts which undermine the power of the priests and destroy our faith in ceremonies, will succeed, and we have reason to tremble." Many, I know, have thus been rescued. Press on in your work. It is of God. C. F.

Of colportage *as an aid to the ministry* in the evangelization of our land, a layman of spirit as gentle as that of the beloved disciple thus speaks: In the conduct of colportage as superintendent and as a participant in its personal labors, with a knowledge of its practical working from the beginning, I cannot doubt it was raised up in the church and ordained of God as a principal coadjutor of the ministry in the evangelization of our country. Over our land are scattered those of every variety of religious opinion, from the simplest Christian faith to the most absurd infidel error—all creeds and sects, to but few of whom any one of the others can be useful, because of the recognized differences and disbeliefs that separate them. But colportage finds its laborers welcomed by many, courteously received and listened to by almost all. "With no creed but the Bible, and no insignia but the cross," it approaches very nearly in form and spirit the example of the Saviour and his immediate disciples, who, rendering unto God and to Cæsar their appropriate homage, "went about doing good." This catholic and cardinal feature of the work, characterizing it from the beginning, illustrates divine wisdom in its origin, and wonderfully adapts it to supply the destitutions of a mixed population in need of the gospel. The Christian church to-day needs an army of ordained missionaries for distant and destitute regions, and yet has not enough to fill its pulpits already established; and with the large ratio of increase in our population, when will it ever overtake and supply this want of an educated ministry? The perishing multitude cannot await their coming. But colportage provides a remedy; it drafts its laborers from the rank and file of all the churches, from a myriad of soldiers, among whom thousands may be found to obey the summons and go forth, not to fill pulpits, but yet to preach Jesus; in the house, by the way, to one, to many, to all who can be reached by visit, or voice, or printed page, so that none, if the church so willed it, need long remain without the gospel. Its economy commends it. It employs humble laymen, known, beloved, and welcomed by those among whom they labor; they ask only for "food and raiment," and are "therewith content." Many of them have homes of their own, and seem especially raised up by Providence and directed to their particular work. By such means the gospel can be carried to the masses of the destitute and neglected, under favorable circumstances for doing them good, and at little cost.

In the history of the past, there has never been a time when the tendency of the Christian church was so cordially towards union of heart and effort for the spread of the gospel. The great army of the church, though marshalled in different divisions, are recognizing more fully one governing object under our great Leader. In colportage they have at their disposal a union missionary agency, providentially provided, approved and beloved, which, coöperating with the Christian ministry, furnishes the means for the speedy and complete evangelization of the destitute masses of our population, and the redemption of our country from its heavy and increasing burdens, the fruit of irreligion and crime. O. D. G.

The origin and practical working of colportage is presented by one who has spent years in collecting means for its prosecution, and observed its usefulness.

In early times the gospel was propagated by three principal agencies—oral preaching, catechetical instruction, and personal effort. The invention of printing synchronizing with the great Reformation, called into being colportage, the carrying of books from city to city, from town to town, from village to village, and even from house to house, which was soon discovered to be a powerful means of spreading the evangelical doctrines. Colportage then is not a new system, but as old as printing and Protestantism. It is the oldest of all our modern schemes of evangelism. It antedates Sunday-schools, Bible, Tract, and Missionary Societies. In our country it has found a broader field for expansion, and has developed new capabilities of usefulness, combining several distinct elements of power. The colporteur is not only a bookseller and tract distributor, but a Bible reader, a lay preacher, and a personal laborer for Christ.

"There is our pastor," said an intelligent layman; "he preaches good, well-studied, and powerful sermons; but his studies leave him but little time for pastoral work among the people. And there is Brother H——, a colporteur of the American Tract Society. He goes out with his wagon-load of tracts and books, calling at every house. He talks with the people, in his plain, earnest way, about personal religion, reads the Bible to them, and offers a short prayer. He goes over this whole parish, over the town, the country, just in that way. He is a 'house-to-house' preacher. And none can doubt that he, and such as he, are doing a vast amount of good for the country and for the cause of Christ."

This is the distinctive mission of the American Tract Society—to send these house and wayside preachers into every part of the land. There is room enough for this special agency, and there is no lack of opportunity. W. V. C.

The power of colportage, as an auxiliary, is thus presented by one who, in the spirit of Harlan Page, has devoted his entire energy to its expansion for more than a score of years:

From my own experience in the work, and from what I have seen and know of its results for more than twenty years, I believe that the system of union missionary colportage embodies a mighty power for good; and if used by the churches of Christ generally in connection with the personal efforts of each individual Christian, under the guidance of faithful pastors, I cannot doubt its adaptation to reach, and with the promised aid of the Holy Spirit, speedily to evangelize the millions of our outlying and destitute population. May the Lord greatly succeed every effort to increase and extend the efficiency of this blessed enterprise. S. W. S.

The writer of the following has not only labored in the colporteur work from its origin, but was one of the instruments, in the hands of God, in its origination. He had prosecuted with large success the "volume enterprise"— the effort to supply churches and pastors with evangelical libraries in which the Society was engaged from 1837 to 1841, and saw, as did others, that this work left a large proportion of the families, and the most needy ones, unsupplied, and hence that some system of missionary visitation must be devised which would reach them. When the work commenced, its first colporteurs were placed under his care, and he has superintended the enterprise over four states ever since.

After enumerating the need and the toils of the work on his field, he gives many instances of rich blessing, and adds: A German colporteur, who labored for many years successfully in Cincinnati, afterwards became a minister, and gathered a church of more than five hundred communicants on the field of his former labors, and is now its faithful pastor. As I recall the names and labors of more than twelve hundred colporteurs who have been connected with this agency for a longer or shorter period of time during the last twenty-five years, I rejoice that the evidence of the grace of God in their hearts and his blessing upon their labors is so abundant. Many who have devoted a few months or years to the colporteur work have been led to a more entire consecration of their lives to the spiritual good of their race, have sought college and seminary learning, and are now preaching the gospel. Some have finished their work on earth, and rest from their labors.

S. W.

One who, with a quick eye to discern and a warm heart to appreciate the need of such an agency, has prosecuted the work with a quiet and persistent energy for twenty years, gives a full sketch of the states over which his superintendency reaches, and urges the value of the work from its *aggressive character:*

Indifference to Christ and his claims is the great cause of the slow progress of Christianity. Men, like the soldiers at the foot of the cross, are utterly careless and regardless of his sufferings for them. Churches stand within sight of their doors, the gospel is faithfully and earnestly preached, but they hear it or heed it not. Men do not want the gospel, else our churches would overflow. These careless ones are the subjects of colportage. The truth must be carried to them and pressed upon them, and they must be *pulled out of the fire.* To this work we have on my field devoted nearly five hundred years of Christian labor, have made a million and a half of Christian family visits, and have put into the hands of the people nearly four millions of volumes of pungent truth, accompanied by constant effort for their salvation. Great and most blessed have been the results; but this aggressive work will be needed so long as the multitudes fail to come to the house of God. H. N. T.

Our remaining witness under this head, laboring in the Northwest, speaks with the intense earnestness with which he works; and no man whose soul is not on fire with love to Christ can work as he does. Combining good judgment, strong faith, and vehement energy, he has met with large and increasing success. His statement is most impressive:

In the fall of 1842, I was introduced to the Tract House at 150 Nassau-street, New York, and was informed that my home would be with Secretaries Hallock and Eastman, then living in adjoining houses, while I should study the documents of the Society and prepare a discourse embodying my views of *the importance of religious reading* as a means of grace, and the work of the American Tract Society in giving that means of grace to our own country and the world.

Seventeen years of my life have been devoted to this service, during which time I have labored in twelve states and travelled about one hundred thousand miles, of which about forty thousand were traversed with a horse and buggy over the prairies of the West, extending into Kansas, Nebraska, and Minnesota. Many thousands of families have been visited at their firesides, business men have been consulted at their offices, and pastors in their studies, making in all not far from one hundred thousand personal visits. Every phase of society has passed in review, and all classes and conditions of men have been visited at their own homes. As the result of all these labors, the following conclusions have grown and become established in my mind:

1. Colportage is *a necessity* in this country. The larger portion of the population, in almost every section, have no identification with the established means of grace, and most of these careless millions never enter any place of worship. Many thousands of families live beyond the reach of all church organizations, where they *cannot*, if they would, attend church; while in the villages and small cities, where two or more churches of different denomina-

tions are started, there is great mutual jealousy of proselytism, whereby both pastors and people are restrained from searching after the careless and the wandering. There is, therefore, a necessity for some agency, auxiliary to the organized churches, which can go to *all men in Jesus' name,* and whose *duty* it shall be to go to every one. I have often travelled over miles by hundreds without finding any place where a religious book could be bought. Bookselling is followed for its profits, and cannot be sustained where there are few people to buy. These vast destitutions of religious reading must therefore continue so long as the population of so large a portion of our country is but from three to twelve persons to the square mile, and so long as there shall remain millions of acres unoccupied.

Without attempting to give definite figures, I feel sure that at this present time not one half of the families in this great Northwest could find a place where to buy a religious book, except the Bible, without travelling a journey, the time and expense of which would amount to the cost of a very fair family library. Add to this the ignorance and carelessness of these masses in respect to everything pertaining to their souls' interest, and you will not wonder that only one-seventh of the population are numbered among the people of God ; and you will see in these moral desolations the absolute necessity for some such agency as colportage to reach the people at their own firesides, and "compel them to come in."

There still remains unoccupied territory stretching off fifteen hundred miles westward to the Pacific, south to Mexico, and north to the British possessions, making perhaps two millions of square miles, tillable and unoccupied. A mighty tide of immigration flows from the settlements into these vast wildernesses continually. I am to-day laboring among six millions of people, where but twenty years ago there were only about two millions. I have chased the frontiers of civilization westward over two hundred miles, and gave it up when they took one grand stride of five hundred miles to the golden mountains of Colorado. What but a ministry "settled on horseback" can meet the necessities of such a country? When will the floating, ever-increasing millions of these wide wastes be supplied with religious reading, if they wait for the location of a bookseller within reach? Surely as a fireside lay agency, colportage is an absolute necessity in these vast fields, and must, in the nature of the case, continue to be a necessity until the country shall become well settled.

2. Union missionary colportage is particularly *adapted to the sparse populations* of our new settlements. I have travelled hundreds of miles where families were so scattered that a congregation of fifty persons could scarcely anywhere be gathered, even though all the families within five miles were to assemble. Among these multitudes I have labored from house to house and from man to man, at the fireside, in the field, the workshop and the office, and on the highways, often meeting with persons who would pour their long pent-up anxieties and solicitudes into my ears, saying, "Sir, you are the first man that ever came to my house to talk to me about eternal things. My soul has been full of doubts and fears, and I have longed for some one with whom to talk. What shall I do to be saved?" I am convinced, from the frequency of these revelations, that the land is full, and always will be full, of persons troubled by the Spirit of God, and anxious for some one to come and lead them to Jesus. The man of God who shall come to such persons in the name of the saving Jesus only, is always a welcome messenger.

I have found in the new settlements that those who had

been identified with the church in their former homes carry with them their denominational prejudices intensified, and when perhaps nine out of every ten such persons would at best give a colporteur of any other branch of the church than their own a cool reception, I have in nine times out of ten met with a kindly and cordial reception and earnest invitation to call again, after the nature of my mission and labors was understood; and this has been the uniform testimony of those associated with me, some of whom have been engaged in denominational labors. Among those never identified with the church, the *catholicity* of this enterprise is a universal commendation often commanding attention when every other consideration fails. Untrammelled by a necessity to defend the tenets of any particular body of believers, the colporteur appears everywhere to plead with men *in Christ's name*, sustained by the *whole force* of the evangelical church, as he persuades them to flee from the wrath to come, and accept mercy, pardon, and eternal life. Avoiding all controversies, the colporteur comes directly to the subject of personal salvation, and pleads with men to be reconciled to God. Having no interest in profits from the sale of books, he recommends those best calculated in every case to compass the end of salvation or edification, and sells books only and always as a means of grace. Being himself fully and heartily converted to God and consecrated to his service, he wastes no time and sacrifices no friendships or interests by pleading the advantages of this or that branch of the church, but heartily commends every one to be fully persuaded in his own mind, and works with equal satisfaction with any and all who love the Lord Jesus. Having himself escaped the snare of the fowler and found peace in believing, and carrying always about with him the dying of the Lord Jesus, he goes to every man in Christ's stead to plead for his best, his eternal interests. Appreciating the danger and the only way of salvation, he exemplifies the true beneficence of the gospel in his own person, and by his zeal and earnestness confounds infidelity, commands confidence and sympathy, and *conquers success everywhere.* Thus the adaptation of *union colportage* to the universal wants of this sparse, headlong, and godless people, is demonstrated.

3. The wide range and blessed *results* of our work are most cheering. It has always been a source of unbounded satisfaction to me to read and study the publications of this Society, and feel and be able to say, without the least hesitation or reserve, here is sound, reliable, practical religious instruction, exactly adapted to the great purposes of religious reading. I have personally canvassed villages, cities, towns, and counties, and systematically supplied every family with something, from a tract to a pastor's library. I have enjoyed the coöperation of pastors, who have visited with me every family within three to six miles of their churches. I have found families in the wildernesses of Missouri and Iowa whose only reading was the religious books or tracts obtained from colporteurs of this Society in some eastern or southern state; and I have found missionaries in the great West who have swept their fingers over the Pastor's Library, saying, "There is where I learned my theology." I have visited thousands of men in the camps and hospitals of our armies, and circulated, personally and with the aid of those associated with me, many hundreds of thousands of these publications among the soldiers.

I know that these laborers and distributions have extended to all varieties of settlements and to all classes of people. They have been among the miners of Michigan, Illinois, and Missouri; in the pineries of Wisconsin and

Minnesota; upon the rafts, flat-boats, and steamboats of our rivers, and the steamboats and shipping of our lakes; and in the pioneer settlements along the rivers and in the prairies and timber of all the northwestern states. They have been into the homes of the rich and the poor, the mansions of the masters, and the cabins of the slaves. These publications have been sown broadcast in all parts of the land, and are often found to be the only reading in the house, and constituting one great staple in the religious influences among the people. Some of the results may be noted.

The demand for aid to Sabbath-schools has always been large, and of late years rapidly on the increase. Some of the colporteurs find their time largely occupied in organizing new schools, and visiting and encouraging old ones and replenishing their libraries. They are instructed to do what they can to encourage schools where they find them, and to organize schools where none exist within practicable distance; and nearly all of them report every quarter more or less schools organized or assisted. We regard this as one of the important branches of our work never to be overlooked.

In accordance with our instructions, with which we are fully in sympathy, it is always a duty in which we find hearty delight, to encourage and aid missionaries and all ministerial brethren who have need of our assistance, in their pastoral and fireside labors. Hence our records show long lists of grants to these brethren, and our files contain many most cherished words of gratitude and encouragement. We regret that the disposition and ability to use the press in their work are so little developed, and that the value of the press as an evangelical help is so little appreciated by many brethren, but rejoice in a growing interest in that direction.

One of the natural fruits of our labors in these pioneer districts is the organized church. A colporteur establishes a prayer-meeting or a Sabbath-school in a log-cabin in a new settlement, where there are perhaps six to ten or twenty families. He watches over and nourishes the spark he has kindled, until, in a few months or years, he has the satisfaction of seeing there established a church and a flourishing congregation. But there are so many elements working together for and in the creation of a church, that we can seldom say that we have accomplished such an organization; yet there are many cases in the aggregate where churches have grown up directly and immediately in connection with the labors of the colporteurs. Thus one reported last year three churches on his field as owing their existence to the labors of colporteurs who preceded him. Another found himself engaged in a series of meetings which grew out of his fireside and public labors. A clergyman was called in to conduct the meetings, and the result was the organization of a church.

I am fully persuaded that the efficient working of the plan of colportage, as now conducted, must necessarily be much more fruitful in Sabbath-schools and prayer-meetings and churches, than it has heretofore been.

A direct tendency of faithful colporteur labors is to revivals. I enjoyed once the company of a pastor with me as I went from house to house among his people. Baxter called successfully to the careless sinners, and Alleine alarmed their slumbering consciences. A demand soon arose for meetings, which were appointed and followed up. The result was, an addition of about one hundred members to that church. One member of that church has continued to support a colporteur ever since. I was informed that another revival followed the visitations and labors in another district. On one occasion I witnessed the evident outpouring of the Spirit and the conversion of a soul, in the presentation of our cause on Sabbath morning. There began a work of grace which extended into the neighboring country, and consumed my time in daily and nightly services for six weeks, hundreds crowding to the services.

There is no more animating, thrilling, glorious, and fruitful service than this fireside searching for souls, with the aid of the combined power of the best men in history. I gave the "Call" to a young man, and at midnight he cried aloud to God for mercy, and sent for his pastor, who led him to Jesus. I sold Nelson to a gentleman for a friend of his, who was thereby saved. Another told me that Nelson's "Cause and Cure" led both himself and his friend to the Saviour. Another narrated to me the cases of six men, in like manner converted by this same book, bought from a colporteur. Another, too ill to leave his bed, sent for a colporteur laboring in his vicinity, to tell him that he owed his hope in Jesus to a book and tract left at his house years before by a colporteur. One writes to me just now, saying, "The first tract I ever saw was the means of my conversion. I have now labored for twenty-five years in the prayer-meeting and Sabbath-school, and other years in the service of this Society where I have made seven thousand three hundred and seventy-three family visits, in nearly every one of which I had religious conversation. I have talked and prayed from morning to night, week in and week out, until I became hoarse and worn out." Another says, "I left home a week ago to preach to one of my Sabbath-schools. The interest became so great, I was obliged to stay the entire week. Oh, what a work the Lord has done in so short a time! Many backsliders have been reclaimed and sinners converted."

But why enumerate. Every month brings us blessed tidings of souls converted. One man has such power with God and with men in his work, that his victories and triumphs are constant. *I am satisfied that conversions have averaged at least five for each year of colporteur labor in this field. Praise God, from whom all blessings flow.*

4. It is my clear conviction, after twenty-four years of observation, study, and experience in this great work, that the system of union missionary colportage possesses an inherent power under God, which, properly cherished, used, and developed by the church of Christ, must be a most efficient auxiliary of the church, leading to and resulting in the bringing of the knowledge of Christ to the people, and identifying them with the established means of grace. This system takes the young men of our institutions of learning, and gives them, during their vacations, a practical training, in personal contact with the people and in the study of practical religious books, of perhaps more value to them in preparation for the pastoral charge than any other equal portions of the whole course. It takes a portion of the lay talent of the church, lying in part or wholly undeveloped, and employs it, not only for the profitable investment of itself, but in such a manner as to bring out and set into proper activity for the cause of God much more of the similarly buried talents of the church. It goes into all the ramifications of society, and diffuses among all classes the personal influence of faithful and zealous fireside labors, stimulating and rousing to action the dormant affections and energies of believers. It plants in every family a suitable religious literature, annually renewing the supply, forestalling evil, directing the tastes aright, laying foundations in righteousness, and erecting a barrier against the tides of delusion that come continually sweeping over the land, threat-

ening to prostrate all landmarks and to desolate the churches. It establishes in these practical works and the recurring faithful visits and prayers of the colporteur a permanent and efficient influence for good, always present and auxiliary to a faithful ministry. Thus much it can be relied upon to do for the church, while for the world it carries the gospel literally to every creature, according to the plan and command of the Saviour, and is therefore in sympathy and coöperation with him, and may be expected to receive, as it has enjoyed hitherto, his blessing. It brings the gospel to man in its essential aspects, without local, sectional, or ecclesiastical prejudices, and commands the attention, interest, and confidence of those outlying masses, pointing them directly and only to Jesus and his salvation.

This plan, expressed in the language of our times, is *union colportage.* With a body of devoted laymen of sound mind and practical judgment, equal in number to the counties of our country, or to an average population of twenty-five thousand, furnished with an adequate supply of practical religious books adapted to all classes, counselled, encouraged, and used by pastors and the churches, it seems that the whole mass of the people might have the gospel brought to them, in the Sabbath-school, prayer-meetings, and personal visitations, within a few years.

G. W.

TESTIMONY OF RETIRED LABORERS.

A minister in high position in the church, who labored in Virginia in 1842, testifies: "The catholic nature of my work gave me access to all denominations, and secured the confidence and coöperation of good people generally. Colportage, conflicting with no good work, aids every other agency. I look back with tender and precious memories to the years devoted to this work." S. B. S. B.

A beloved pastor writes: "I thank God that I was permitted to invest thirteen years in this work, laboring either as a general agent or a superintendent of colportage. I traversed repeatedly Indiana and Northern Ohio, and to some extent Maryland, Illinois, Michigan, Wisconsin, Iowa, Missouri, Arkansas, Mississippi, and Louisiana; and now, after an interval of nearly five years spent in a blessed pastorate, it is pleasant in imagination to revisit those wide fields, and live over again the stirring scenes of the tract agency. I would testify, as in the sight of God, to the following points:

1. *The work sought to be accomplished was greatly needed.* In all those states there was widespread spiritual destitution. Vast numbers of families were without any religious reading, without stated preaching, neither reached, nor likely for a long time to be reached, by the ordinary means of evangelization. The more systematically and thoroughly we explored, the more extensive and startling were the destitutions revealed. Facts of the most humiliating and alarming character were developed. Wide districts were found in which "the people sat in great darkness;" while in townships and counties supposed to be well supplied,

our brethren going from house to house discovered hundreds of families as destitute of good books and other gospel appliances as those living in the wilds of Africa. It was apparent also, that in order to reach these destitute ones, the people generally must be visited.

2. *The truly catholic spirit and aim of the work* everywhere commended it to the piety and the common sense of the people. The more thoroughly they understood just what the Tract Society was trying to do and how, the more heartily all who loved Christ, and all good citizens, bade it God-speed. I never visited a place of any importance where there were not individuals ready to rise up and bear testimony to the adaptation of colportage to meet wants existing in their own immediate neighborhood. Said an excellent pastor in his pulpit: "If there is in all the land a work suited to the present religious wants of the people—a work conceived and carried out in the very spirit of the gospel, it is this book-missionary work of the Tract Society." And thousands of times did I hear substantially the same sentiments expressed privately.

3. *The blessing of God* so attended the work, that it was remarkably successful. I know of no evangelizing enterprise that has been more successful. God only can tell in what great variety and how widely it has diffused enlightening and saving influences. It has carried spiritual food to many a famishing child of God, and spiritual light and life to many a sinner, who otherwise would have died without a knowledge of the Saviour. The ignorant have been instructed, the backslider reclaimed, the careless awakened, the convicted led to Christ, and the dying prepared for the great change. Thus it has been the occasion of stirring up many to pray, and furnished the means by which many a prayer has been signally answered. It has

done much to counteract skepticism and infidelity. It has sowed the seed of Sabbath-schools, churches, and other permanent gospel institutions, widely over the country. Almost everywhere its quiet, blessed influence has been felt, if not realized. Like the silent, genial influence of the sunshine and showers, it has moved multitudes of human minds and hearts by the sweet but mighty forces of light and love; and while aiding all other Christian efforts, it has hindered none. No laborer for Christ and souls can ever rise up and say that at any time, or in any place, this work of union colportage has proved injurious to any other good work. While its results have to a great extent blended with the results of all other Christian influences, and thus been lost to our view, the history of this work is written indelibly in the memories, consciences, and character of immortal beings. Could all that has resulted, directly or indirectly, from this enterprise be at once annihilated, and every thing be put back just as it otherwise would have been, a most startling and calamitous change would be witnessed—a change that would open all eyes to the great and wonderful good which God has accomplished through this humble agency.

4. I see no reason why this system of union colportage, coöperating with the churches, may not still be employed with blessed results, till the whole land shall be completely evangelized. It combines two great elements of power—personal Christian effort and the press. The press is certainly to be employed more and more extensively to spread the truths of the gospel. It cannot be questioned that private Christians must continue to go forth as gospel seed-bearers, and that they must have a more active, working, missionary spirit, before the gospel will triumph throughout the land. Who then can doubt that a combination of these two great elements of moral

power, in some form, is to be employed more extensively and successfully, till the world shall have been converted? This method of spreading everywhere the truths of the gospel, by private Christians going from house to house, and calling the attention of all classes to the invitations and warnings of God's word, and with prayer to God entreating the people to give attention to their soul's salvation, is in strict accordance with the commands of Christ, the practice of the apostles, and the spirit of Christianity. If, in connection with this going forth bearing precious seed, there shall be more of the loving, praying, weeping spirit which God so highly esteems—more of spontaneous, volunteer, Christ-like effort, and less hired labor, unquestionably the results will be more blessed and abundant." S. W.

A minister of great energy and executive ability, now in the pastorate, writes: It was my privilege to engage as a student in colportage in the summer of 1846, after which I devoted many years to its prosecution. Interest deepened with experience and personal knowledge of the needs of the people. Everywhere the work was needed, in every place it was adapted, in every place where suitable men were employed it was blessed, often presenting *all the points of successful evangelization*—supplying the destitute with the means of grace, and securing the blessing of the Spirit in the conversion of souls, thus creating the *material* for churches, stimulating education, promoting intelligence and the observance of the Sabbath, temperance, and general good order and thrift.

What is thus quickly and conscientiously said, was not so quickly or easily learned; but the facts having been laboriously gathered, nothing can rob them of their power over my mind and heart. The wisest planning of the best hearts and heads developes the fundamental necessity in our times and country for *loving, and faithful, and capable personal work* accompanying and enforcing the teachings of *evangelical truth in some of its printed forms.*

As an agency for evangelization, combining in a simple and effective manner these great elements of power, Union Colportage is still the great need of this country, not as a substitute for the ministry or the organized church, but as a pioneer and then as a supplementary work, for which there is a field almost everywhere.

As a general coöperating agency, hindering none and helping all others which are built upon and employ the truth as it is in Jesus; as a promoter of individual awakening and conversion, of revivals and Christian edification, a help to the ministry, and the trusted auxiliary of all working Christians, bringing aid when and where most needed, strengthening hands and hearts ready to fail without the timely and practical relief—we gratefully point to a long and never-to-be-obliterated record with which we have been personally familiar, and over which the heart has often been lifted in thanksgiving to God. It is a blessed way of reaching and saving the millions of our land, who must perish if not sought out by earnest men of God, who carry a revival of religion in their hearts and the saving truths of the gospel in their hands.

The land is flooded with infidel, frivolous, and vicious books and periodicals. Preoccupy the ground with an attractive Christian literature by the most aggressive means, or the nation is cursed. None but the *most aggressive* means will do the work. Delay not, falter not; reiterate the claims of the masses; proclaim the efficacy of *personal effort* aided by the press; fill the land with itinerant gospel carriers and workers; call upon the people of God to pray and give, to employ the press at home, and let the

leaves of the tree of life be spread before every ignorant or indifferent mind. God bless the Tract Society, and its noble system of colportage. Y. H.

No man living better understands the working of colportage, or has been more devoted to its expansion, than the writer of the following; and few have gathered such abundant results:

In the fall of 1844, God led me to labor for one year as a colporteur of the American Tract Society. From that to the close of 1865, with the exception of four months, my whole time was given to this work in some of its departments. I have traversed western Pennsylvania, Maryland, Virginia, North Carolina, South Carolina, and some portions of Georgia, besides numerous excursions in other states. As to the need of colportage over this vast field, the thousands of families without Bibles or books of any kind who have been visited and supplied, the seventy-five thousand children brought into Sabbath-schools, many of whom by this means received their first book and learned their first lesson—is enough to satisfy the most skeptical. I have found thousands of families who had never seen a preacher in their houses, never heard a chapter of God's word read, or a prayer offered. I have often heard children between eight and eighteen years old, when on our knees, call out, "Dad, (or mam,) what is that man doing?" and they would sometimes run out crying or laughing, and peep in at us between the logs of the cabin.

While the number of families entirely destitute of religious books is greatly reduced, still hundreds have but a small supply. New families are constantly springing up that must be supplied in the same way, or die in ignorance and sin. Such is the broken and almost impassable condition of large portions of the field over which I have labored, that at least one generation must pass into eternity before the people will be able to supply themselves with the stated means of grace—churches, pastors, books, and schools.

While there are many portions of this field as well supplied with ministers, churches, and books, as any in our country, still I know of no place where an intelligent, prudent man of God might not do great good by preaching and distributing books and tracts from house to house. I am very certain that tracts are still read with more interest than they ever have been. I have often been told by intelligent men that they have no time to read a book through, but they read all the tracts which come in their way. Not long since, I had to wait four hours for a conveyance in a little village, where a number were drinking and swearing. There were three grog-shops well filled with customers, in all stages of intoxication. In one hour I had said a few words to, and put a tract in the hands of every person I could find. I remained two hours after, but did not hear another oath. One man said he had not "*took in*" that much religion for years.

I have never found any community where there were not some families who attended no place of worship and could say, No man cares for our souls. Few pastors are able to meet the demands made on them by their own people; consequently those who don't go to church are left to perish in their sins. They are neglected, for fear that those who visit them should be suspected as proselyters. As a general rule, a stranger can do them more good than those who know them. To all classes who neglect the house of God, colportage is peculiarly adapted. The physician examines his patient, and then makes his prescription: this is just what the colporteur does. If he finds an infidel, he gives him Nelson's "Cause and Cure;" if a hardened sinner, Baxter's "Call," or something similar; to a Sabbath breaker, a Sabbath manual; and so on through the whole catalogue of sinners, he has a prescription for every one. At least one out of every four counties over all the vast field I have explored stands in crying need of a pious, godly colporteur of the Tract Society.

The actual results of this kind of labor have proved it to be a most successful, as well as a most economical system of doing good. The first man I ever employed as colporteur had been a circuit preacher sixteen years. At the close of his first year of this work, he told me he believed he had accomplished more real good in that year than in the sixteen previous years. He said he had been preaching to a people without any books, and when converted they did not *stick;* but now, said he, they *stick*, as a general rule, well.

It is the only way a large class can be supplied with a religious literature. One half the people have never seen a book-store, and many who are able to buy never will, while thousands are utterly unable. By carrying religious books to them, we forestall a vicious literature, and prepare the way for all other good influences to follow. They are John the Baptists going before, crying, "Prepare ye the way of the Lord, make his paths straight;" and they turn many to righteousness. It is a thorough way to gather all the children into Sabbath-schools. It greatly aids ministers in their work to carry in their pockets a variety of tracts. In protracted meetings they are like the gentle rain that follows the shower, percolating into the earth. The sermons are the showers which rouse the feelings, reading tracts during the recesses impresses the truth deeper into the soul, and acts more directly on the judgment.

If all the different branches of the church which preach and teach the very truths taught by the Tract Society would unite their efforts in this Society, a colporteur could be employed for every two counties in our country, without interfering with any denominational enterprise. Oh that the day may soon come when the prayer of Jesus Christ may be answered, that his people may all be one in coöperation, as he and the Father are one in fact. J. C.

Not a few of the most godly and successful foreign missionaries commenced their active work for Christ in this home missionary agency. Their estimate of its adaptation to the destitute, both at home and abroad, is based upon actual experiment and wide observation. Of this class, a few words well embody the general judgment of all.

One racily describes his experience in the earlier days of the work, in a field near to the city of New York, and then adds: From personal experience, gained week after week from house to house, I am constrained to think that no pastor or church-member knows the condition of the community in which he resides, unless he has engaged in some such labor; and whether engaged in by pastor or colporteur, or better, by pastor and layman and colporteur combined, such labors are of inestimable advantage, and constitute the hope of the church militant. This spirit carries the gospel to other lands; and when the gospel is planted there, this spirit sets native colporteurs at work there as leaven, without which the lump cannot be leavened.

Representing no local sect, no narrow circle, no single church or land, through these undying works breathes and lives again the highest consecration of past ages.

Thomas à Kempis and Baxter, Luther and Edwards, D'Aubigné and Brainerd, Martyn, McCheyne, and Judson—*all Christ's*, and now saints in heaven, still plead. Stirring up no personal antagonism, awaking no present prejudices, this still printed voice comes with the hushed whisper of the mighty past, and quietly tells the infidel his sophism, the impenitent his guilt; and they can quarrel neither with the body in the grave nor the soul in the bosom of God.

As a stranger, the colporteur finds no sectarian opposition. Churches, pastors, elders, Sabbath-schools, parents, welcome an ally, and press him into a common work. Aged mothers in Israel put on their spectacles and gaze upon the fresh page, hallowed by the genius of the well-known dead. Those unused to prayer allow the stranger to kneel and pray for them, and often reveal the hidden want of their souls to one whom they regard as a messenger from God. Little children at the roadside, going home from school, gaze at the illustrated Scripture stories; and then sometimes the sunny smile of the child melts the parent's icy soul. When the narrative written for a child has made the strong man a child, the entering wedge is found, and gospel truth may be driven home through what had been most fixed and knotted opposition.

Meantime the young theological student is learning human nature, and being fitted for future work. As he marks and ponders the puerile and absurd sophisms which seem trusted bulwarks for infidels and universalists, he recognizes the stubbornness of that opposition to God which in so defenceless a position can maintain so prolonged and desperate a resistance. While he meets the lowly, and by his lips "to the poor the gospel is preached," he finds a growing union with Him who had compassion on the sheep without a shepherd. May God bless the American Tract Society a hundred-fold, and make its pages leaves of healing for all nations.

D. W. M.

Since the following was written, its lamented author has been called "up higher." We cannot doubt his testimony even now would be the same.

I would testify most explicitly to the *reflex influence* of colportage on those who are permitted to engage in it, especially such as are preparing to preach the gospel, either at home or abroad. The theological student who spends his vacations in active colportage, recruits his health, strengthens his body, acquires a practical acquaintance with human nature, a knowledge of the various forms and devices of error, and skill in meeting them, a sympathy with the poor and ignorant, and facility of accommodating himself to their circumstances, and a habit of enduring hardship and practising self-denial which can be attained in no other way. I question whether there be any one branch of instruction in the whole theological course more valuable to the pastor than this experience. But to the missionary in foreign lands and among the degraded heathen, such a preparation is still more helpful. This has been my own experience; and since my return to this country, having been repeatedly asked by candidates for the ministry what *special preparation* was needed, or what *extra branches* should be studied to fit one for the foreign field, I have often replied that I knew of no other branch of study, not included in the regular seminary course, which would be so useful as this. Would it not be well if our ecclesiastical bodies, in their examination of candidates for ordination, should insist on some such practical course of labor as a necessary preparation for the highest usefulness in the pastoral office? J. E. F.

Another missionary writes: "As to the general good influence of the training secured by colporteur service, I am very positive: I have always looked back to that experience as one of the best of my life. I think I never more directly and simply served God than in my colporteur labors." This gentleman is occupying one of the most responsible positions in the church.

One who prefers to work through ecclesiastical organizations, where this can be done, thus speaks of his colporteur labors: It was the only practical training which I had before I entered the ministry, and without something of the kind, my increasing conviction is that no man ought to be ordained. Colporteur work was to me a development of that dormant side of the student—how to use one's weapons. He gets the armor in college and seminary; but if he goes forth to battle with it without putting it to the proof, he will be sure to make mistakes. In the missionary work, we are colporteurs as well as preachers and teachers. I seldom left my house without a bundle of tracts, and often tried the plan which I had learned as a colporteur, and was more bold to undertake for Christ from my former experience. J. K. W.

We close these extracts with the well-considered thoughts of one who, for the last ten years, has been an honored pastor in the West. His cordial and earnest words reveal the great heart in his bosom, which beats so warmly with love for souls.

If there are any years of my life on which I look back with delight; if there has been any period in which I was of use in the Master's service; if there are any remembrances precious beyond the power of language to express, they grew out of the agency I was permitted to perform for the American Tract Society. Of the many impressions received never to be effaced, I note,

1. One thing that from the first and all along gave me great assurance, was the *gradual providential development* of the work. It was not a beautiful scheme of man's devising, perfected at once, like a manufactory, all its machinery perfected before a single thread is spun; or like a gallant ship, all her rigging adjusted and her sails set before she leaves the harbor. To illustrate what I mean: When the lamented Dr. Porter, in a private parlor incidentally suggested to a few friends, that if a large edition of some book or tract were printed, it might be obtained for a less sum than they had been accustomed to pay, and so gratuitous circulation would be facilitated, who but the all-seeing Eye discerned that out of that suggestion would grow the present world-wide enterprise of the American Tract Society?

When the idea was started—we know not in whose mind it originated; we would fain believe that it was a scintillation from the throne of God—but when the idea was started in 1832 that it was desirable to place one or more religious tracts in every accessible family between lake Erie and New Orleans, who would have predicted as the result the kindling of that zeal which has placed already so many millions of such tracts in the dwellings of this land?

When four Christian men in 1828 gave eight hundred dollars to the Society for the purpose of perpetuating "Doddridge's Rise and Progress of Religion in the Soul," the first book printed by the Society—fit harbinger of the issues that should follow—who would have ventured the prediction that in forty years a single organization would have conveyed to the families in this country more than twenty millions of such books? We believe they are to be found in every inhabited county and district of these United States.

When the lamented Evarts, who with "the tenderness of a child that could stoop to the sufferings of the individual combined a love that could belt the globe," urged upon the Society the duty of publishing the gospel in foreign and pagan lands, he did not venture to express the hope that in so short a time the people of one hundred and forty languages and dialects should read, "in their own tongues wherein they were born, the wonderful works of God."

And when a young man, so unnoticed and unknown that his name probably will be scarcely heard among men, cried out almost in anguish, "I cannot live so; I cannot stand it any longer: you send me out to sell these books; but I call on one family after another, one family after another, who have not a single picayune to buy with; I converse with them and pray with them, but I leave them as destitute of truth on the printed page as I found them; and I cannot live so; I cannot stand it any longer; and unless you can devise some way by which I may give the gospel to the poor without money and without price, I must stop;" an indifferent listener would scarcely out of this longing to supply the destitute have elaborated the method and the results, as witnessed by us, of union colportage.

From such small beginnings, from such incidental suggestions, the work of the Society has extended all over this land. "Behold how great a matter a little fire kindleth!" But it needed to be kindled by the love and fanned by the breath of the Spirit of God.

2. A personal acquaintance with a great many of those laborers furnished delightful evidence of the power of divine grace to produce a truly enlarged and benevolent charity. Though born in different lands, speaking different tongues, and associated with many different communions, there was great unity of sentiment and experience as to what is essential to salvation. Rarely in their labors and in their colporteur conventions would a word be spoken to the prejudice of any Christian brother. My conviction that all true Christians are one, was constantly deepened by the observation of more than fifteen years in connection with the work of colportage.

3. Another fact, giving assurance of success in prosecuting colportage, is the character of the publications. It was almost uniformly the case with pastors, when an unusual seriousness pervaded their congregations, to say to me, "Cannot you send to me a package of tracts?" or, "I must have some of the publications of the Society to meet the condition of my people." The grateful conclusion, not to be resisted, was, these pastors know whereof they affirm, and it must be that these publications are eminently suited to promote the spiritual welfare of the people. The complaint has been made that they were not sufficiently denominational to suit some persons; but I do not recall a single instance when it was named as a fault that they were lacking in saving truth. What condition in life is there—what possible trouble of mind, or body, or estate, in which the sufferer may not derive instruction, warning, or consolation, from some of the excellent treatises issued by the Society?

4. How the moral destitutions of this great country can

be better explored, brought to the notice of the church, and supplied with saving truth in a permanent form, than by union colportage, in advance of, and in connection with, the Christian ministry, I do not know. These destitutions are so great, it is difficult to gain any adequate apprehension of them. A residence of more than ten years in the valley of the Mississippi has confirmed me in the impression that this great West presents a field of labor imperative in its demands, glorious in its prospects, and at the same time almost disheartening, because of its vastness. This may to a certain extent be conjectured by the length of the majestic river that runs through its centre, indicated by the variety of temperature its waters encounter in their passage to the gulf. I look out from my window to-day and witness its mighty throes, as if determined to be rid of its bondage of ice. Above us, for a month yet to come, it may quietly wear its chains; while below us, the flowers are in full bloom on its banks; and lower still, the trees have passed through their blossoming, and are well on their way to fruitage. All the distance through these thousands of miles, from its source to its mouth, on either side of it, and far, far back on its prairies, already multitudes of immortal beings are spending their season of probation and forming characters for eternity; and alas, how few comparatively are toiling for their salvation! When our Saviour said to his disciples, "The harvest truly is great, but the laborers are few; pray ye therefore the Lord of the harvest, that he would send forth laborers into his harvest," can it be that his heart of infinite love did not embrace the inhabitants of this vast territory? As the tide of immigration sets so strongly in this direction, so may the facilities for reaching them at their firesides, however far apart, furnished by union colportage, be multiplied a thousand-fold. H. B. H.

OPINIONS OF PASTORS.

A pastor in New York state, of large experience, thus writes: "Next to the preaching of the gospel, colportage, when rightly conducted, has long seemed to me to be the grand instrumentality appointed by the church's Head for the extension of his kingdom. In all parts of our land there are multitudes of people who are utterly overlooked by the ordinary instrumentalities of grace. Under the very shadow of the magnificent churches of the great cities there are thousands who never enter them.

But this agency is specially needed in the sparsely settled portions of the country. In very many places there is an absolute famine of the bread of life. No schools on either week day or Sabbath, no churches accessible, no books, except perhaps some far worse than none, whose tendency is to debase and ruin the morals and the soul, which the emissaries of the spirit of Evil are usually found earnest in disseminating in advance even of the agency of the Tract Society. In such cases, and their name is legion, what can be expected but that Satan will rule supreme, and that the people will perish for lack of knowledge.

Here is the especial field of colportage. Surely it is the duty of the whole church, without regard to denominational distinctions, to send forth faithful laborers to scatter broadcast the good seed of the word throughout all those moral desolations. This is the cheapest, most efficient, and successful instrumentality practicable. To establish churches and give the preached gospel by the living voice wherever humanity is spread, is not possible at the present day. The way must be prepared for the establishment of Messiah's kingdom in such wildernesses of sin by the humble, but invaluable and absolutely necessary labors of the colporteur. Let any one read those wonderful records, "Five Years in the Alleghanies," and "Twenty Years among the Colporteurs," lately published by the Tract Society, and tell me when and where such an incalculable amount of good has ever been effected at so small a cost of money by any other agency. Multitudes of souls, converted to God through the effusion of his Spirit and his blessing on the faithful labors of the colporteurs, many converts brought themselves to be first colporteurs, and afterwards preachers of the gospel; and all this costing less money to the church than is needed to support a single one of the great churches of the land, and not a tithe of what is yearly expended in the support of one of those hotbeds of immorality, our metropolitan theatres.

The power of this agency for the regeneration of the world is incalculable, and it only needs to be rightly employed to make it mighty to the pulling down of the strongholds of sin. It supplies for the people of all classes just the sanctified literature they need, for it gives food for babes and strong meat for the most cultivated intellect and holy heart. It is the true and faithful handmaid of the settled ministry, a handmaid abundantly owned and blessed by the Head of the church. D. M. M.

An honored and useful pastor in New York state, after describing the wonderful effects of the Society's work in his own church, adds: "I cannot but regard the Tract Society as one of the great religious instrumentalities in the providence of God for evangelizing the masses, especially that class who, from various causes, are excluded from regular attendance on the sanctuary."

A pastor, residing in one of the large seaboard towns in Massachusetts, writes: The field I cultivate greatly needs the kind of labor bestowed by the colporteur. It is specially adapted to do unbounded good here. Colportage has been a blessing, not only to the masses outside of the churches and the ministry, but to the churches and the ministry themselves. It has been a universal benefit to this people. We need this day as much as any one means of grace, a living, discreet colporteur. He would do more for home evangelization than any other effort. I often hear the indifferent, the irreligious as well as the Christian, speak of the influence of colportage, as it has been enjoyed in years past in this place. May the time not be distant when we may welcome among us another to help in the great work of saving souls.

A pastor of one of the churches in Maine writes: I have had an opportunity for the past two years to observe the workings of colportage, and I feel that it is an instrumentality which nothing else can supply the place of. Whether in destitute neighborhoods, or coöperating with other agencies, it is of vast value. Of course it is most needed in those places where the gospel is not preached; yet there is great good done by the visitation of those places blessed by a faithful ministry, by conversing with families, seeking out the neglected and remote, and supplying the want of good, sound, wholesome books. The labors of Dea. S. on the broad field he has traversed, have been of exceeding value. His visits have been prized; his books are the seed of a coming harvest, some already gathered. Our land can never be Christianized till men are sought out in the byways and forsaken precincts, and the gospel preached to them by laymen sent forth for this very work. I have no doubts as to the importance and adaptedness of this mode of activity, if you can get men of zeal, and self-denial, and discrimination to engage in this work. There is need of thousands all over our land, who can not only distribute books, but teach and preach wherever they go. Every good pastor and superintendent in our rural districts, or those away from business centres where books can be obtained, rejoice in the visit of the colporteur, and his presence and aid in the school and the prayer-meeting. I need not allude to the value of his visits to the family circle waiting for the supply of just such books as he carries, safe, healthy, and fitted to lift up and purify the heart.

A pastor in M—— writes: While laboring, some years since, at the South, I became impressed with the special usefulness of colportage there, from its peculiar adaptation to the state of the population. In large portions of the South the people are so sparsely settled that colportage seems to be the only agency by which the gospel can reach them. At least, it is an essential agency for covering the large margin of deficiency, after the ordained ministry and all church appliances have done their best. Except at county sites, it is rare that a minister's labors are confined to a single parish; and preaching-places are so far apart that they must be visited in their turn, and on separate Sabbaths. The families are so scattered that very little pastoral visitation is attempted. I found one minister settled at a county site, who, besides ministering to the church where he lived, and teaching at the academy, and keeping a boarding-house, and overseeing a plantation, had three other congregations, which must take their turn on successive Sabbaths, the nearest of which was twelve miles distant; one was twenty-four miles. Though this is an extreme case, yet it illustrates how far short the regular ministry comes, and must of necessity come, of meeting the spiritual wants of the people. Another fact which makes colportage more needed South than in some other portions of the Union is that the South is not so flooded with books, and so overrun with agents of all kinds, consequently the colporteur is welcomed, and his books are gladly received and eagerly read.

A minister of wide experience, in an Eastern state, testifies: Every day's observation increases my conviction that colportage should be largely increased in New England. I would not confine these men to the poorer and more sparsely settled portions of the country. It would pay abundantly to have every part of our country traversed by them, and every family, if possible, visited. Vastly could the influence and the power of the church be augmented by such an agency well chosen, and having the confidence and the coöperation of the people of God. There is not a city or a rural district where the labors of a faithful colporteur would not result in rich harvests of blessing. I doubt if, in a land like this, and during the current year, a half-million of dollars could be more wisely or hopefully employed than in sending into the different parts of our land an army of over a thousand devoted Christian colporteurs. I would love to see so grand an experiment on actual trial. I believe there is a growing conviction of the need of this agency, and of its great value. May friends not be wanting to give it new life and power in this land.

Says another minister: It appears evident to my mind that the church in its organized form cannot speedily reach the multitude scattered on the frontier, in the mountains, and other sparsely-settled portions of our country. To effect the great end of the gospel respecting such communities, we must go back to primitive apostolic plans. They went everywhere preaching the word. Now in twos, now in groups, here perhaps a single one; but all telling of Jesus, his crucifixion, resurrection, and glorious ascension into heaven, and exhorting all to believe in him. Had they possessed the tracts and books of the American Tract Society, I think they would have carried them "to the regions beyond." They would have been faithful and true colporteurs. Colportage goes out as the vanguard of the army of the Lord, as the pioneer of the organized church, preparing the way and selecting appropriate ground for encampments. And when this work is complete, it coöperates with the churches, and everywhere compels attention, induces conviction, reclaims the backslider, guides the inquiring, and through the printed page and the living ministry points all to the Lamb of God which taketh away the sin of the world. S. P. L.

A successful pastor in New Jersey writes: As a pioneer, your Society has done much to awaken the attention of the evangelical churches to existing destitutions, and the facts becoming known have stimulated the churches to explore their outlying and unknown territory, and follow your colporteurs with the more regular, permanent, and systematic ordinances of the gospel.

A pastor of national reputation, large influence, and great success, thus expresses his views: I have felt a particular interest in colportage since it was inaugurated, and all my observation and experience have been constantly raising my estimate of it. While I was at E——, my attention to Northern Pennsylvania satisfied me that it was invaluable and indispensable in agricultural districts; and my work of more than fifteen years in U——, has as fully satisfied me of the need and importance of it in large towns. As a preacher of the gospel, I should not be likely to depreciate the ministry; but it is not the sole agency in the cause for which it performs a preëminent part. Nay, limited and exercised as the ministry is, only the smaller portion of the people are reached by it in the most favored communities. It has long been the distress of many of my brethren that we addressed only our congregations, and that these were constituted by less than one-half or two-thirds of our fellow-citizens. We do not tire of appealing to the same ears, but we long to speak to the multitudes who never listen to us. They will not come to hear us, and if we prepare ourselves to say any thing worth being announced from the pulpit, and give due heed to those who attend to us there, we cannot possibly be talking to others at their homes and places of labor and business. We must have coöperation if the masses are to be evangelized.

It has long been a favorite idea with me that the local churches should make it their mission not to build themselves up, but to Christianize the surrounding population. This is widely regarded as an extra service, or as an incident to the services of the sanctuary, instead of being aimed at primarily and principally. The proper order and progress are reversed. Instead of seeking to bear the gospel to the community, and in this way, and as the result of this, enjoy an enlargement and strengthening of the church, the object is to enlarge and strengthen the church, and to let the community, to some extent, be thus furnished with the gospel. The Saviour does not commission his disciples in any town to make a flourishing organization of the First or Second Presbyterian, or Reformed Dutch, or Congregational, or Methodist, or Episcopal, or Baptist societies; but to take the truth to the inhabitants of that town and to press it upon them; and they ought to associate together, not to form large and wealthy bodies, but to press the truth on every citizen. With such a policy, a church is most sure to prosper. It is a benevolent, instead of a selfish spirit that animates it, and this alone is its true life. It is doing the Lord's work, and not its own, and he may be expected to favor it. The character of the members is improved by it, and they are much more sure to help the fraternity to which they belong. The evangelization of the surrounding population must ordinarily be accomplished, and is ordinarily best accomplished, by the communicants of a church. Comparatively few can afford a paid agency, and it is an inestimable advantage to them to perform it themselves. But there is a great extent of field in the country, for which volunteers cannot be, and certainly will not be enlisted; and the Tract Society may have use for all the means it can command in sending laborers into it, permanent and transient, and laborers who, while doing the needful work for the time being, may induce resident Christians to embark in it.

Earnestly praying for a continued blessing on your Society throughout its wide sphere, and particularly the department of colportage, I am yours, P. H. F.

Our remaining witness, an able and devoted minister in Ohio, writes from personal observation extending over a wide field and for many years: I have watched, with increasing interest, the efforts of the American Tract Society to evangelize the masses by union colportage. At an early day I saw the necessity for such an agency. My home was near a dense country population with small means of grace, and a part of my time was given to a voluntary colportage among them. The Lord blessed the means, and his own work of conversion met me everywhere. At a subsequent period, I was connected with one of our colleges as a professor. The population for miles around was without a ministry of Christ, or a Sabbath-school. An extensive colportage was commenced, and the whole region has been enlightened by this means. Many of the young men have spent their vacations as colporteurs, and filled the country with Sabbath-schools and publications. The contrast between the population of to-day and at that period is marked and wonderful. The change is, in a great measure, due, under God, to this labor.

While in college life and since, I have travelled on religious exploring tours in Ohio, Virginia, Kentucky and Indiana, over fifty thousand miles. A large portion of this on horseback and among our outlying and interlying masses beyond and between the churches, and witnessed, at many points in the South and West, the evangelizing effects of colportage. The moral and religious condition of these masses is, in many places, most melancholy and deplorable. Ignorance, as dense as Egyptian darkness, envelops them. In Ohio we have between one-third and one-fourth of our entire population living and dying without the gospel. In Indiana and Kentucky is a large proportion in the same awful state. Colportage is the only agency by which, at present, they can be evangelized; and this, to be effective, must not be denominational, but union. By all means, let the land be filled with it. In addition to the country round about the college referred to, I am personally acquainted with other sections where the same efforts have been followed with the same blessed results: the darkness has been dissipated, souls converted, Sabbath and day schools introduced, churches organized, and the population redeemed. Blessed be God for such an agency and such results! J. M. E.

Would to God that all our pastors coöperated heartily in this blessed work.

AN ARMY COLPORTEUR DESCRIBED.

BY CHAPLAIN J. E. H.

If one should visit the army of the Potomac, and stay for some time in any part of it, he would be pretty certain to meet an odd little man going round among the boys. He generally has a satchel slung over his shoulder, or a package under his arm, or both; and if you should see him approaching your home, where scenes are peaceful, you would prepare for an interview with an old-fashioned, energetic dealer in some kind of small-wares. His appearance, though not remarkable, excites interest; and you say to yourself, "I wonder what that little man is doing in the army." He is about five feet six inches in height, and of a square-built, chunky frame; he wears a soft felt hat and a brown coat, both of which have done good service; his vest and pants, a little soiled, suggest that he works actively sometimes; his warm shirt, of gray stocking-web, has been selected for comfort rather than for beauty; the paper collar, without any necktie, buttoned carelessly on the shirt, is the only mark about him of any deference to fashion; and the plain, unpolished shoes, which are of the kind that soldiers have, put it beyond denial that the little man is given to walking. His face has a somewhat abstracted expression, yet indicates kind-heartedness, vivacity, humility, and shrewdness. He seems between fifty and sixty years of age; time and care have made furrows on his cheeks, and his dark brown hair is growing thin and sparse. But his eye is bright and restless; and he shoves along with his bundle under his arm, as though he had plenty of business on hand.

Mark him as he enters a camp and is recognized by the soldiers. "Hey, Uncle John, is that you?" says one, who starts to meet him. "How are you, Uncle John?" echoes another from within his tent. "I am glad to see you, Uncle John. Have you any soap to-day?" cries a third; and a fourth nephew inquires, "Uncle John, have you brought the writing-paper and envelopes you promised?" The wide-awake little man is at home among them, and answers in a cheery, lively way, "How are you, dear boys? I'm glad to see you. I guess I've got a little something for you—I was thinking you'd be wanting a little paper and needles, for the paymaster hasn't been round for a good while, has he? Just step up, boys; I can't carry much, you know, but I'll give you what I've got." He is instantly surrounded by a circle of our blue-coated heroes, ready for his little gifts, and yet more ready for what Uncle John may have to say; for they know well that he never finds himself among soldiers without saying something that is worth listening to.

Hark to the merry laughter, as Uncle John makes some singular observation! See the fixed attention, as he relates some stirring news, or interesting incident! Listen to "That's so, Uncle John; that's so," as he renders some excellent sentiment or advice, in his terse, striking way! And all the time both his hands are busy dispensing sheets of paper, and pens, and thread, etc., with skilful and impartial generosity. After these gifts, tracts and religious reading, produced from the black satchel, are distributed to many glad recipients, Uncle John, the meanwhile, continuing his remarks. Now his stock is exhausted; and the little man earnestly repeats an invitation which he has already given incidentally, perhaps half-a-dozen times. "Now boys, do n't forget the prayer-meeting the chaplain is going to have this evening. Come, come, dear boys, and let us ask God to bless us." "We will, Uncle John, we will," is the response of many voices; and possibly the evening hour will show that the invitation has been also accepted by many silent, softened hearts that did not dare to speak. The next moment "Uncle Johnnie 's gone!" but the influences of his genial soul are scattered all around.

The full name of this ubiquitous little man, who has all the soldiers in the army of the Potomac for his nephews, is known to but few of those who are familiar with his countenance and person; but it is a name which is enrolled for everlasting life and honor in the blessed book above. He labors as distributing agent for the Sanitary Commission, and as army colporteur of the American Tract Society, by whom he is supported; but he is so original a genius, and such an active, whole-souled, liberal-hearted philanthropist, that it is difficult to think of him as connected with any particular institution. I was struck with the remark of a colored man, as some were discussing the character of Uncle John: "I'll just tell you, then, what *I* thinks; I thinks *this*—I'thinks Uncle John is a *real Christianity.*" The truth could scarcely be expressed better. While entertaining decided denominational sentiments and attachments, Uncle John labors everywhere with such a largeness of spirit, and such a loftiness of view, that one can regard him only as belonging to the church of God and the religion of Jesus Christ.

The first half of his life was passed in his cousin's brewery, and was thoroughly given to business; but about fifteen years ago God touched the brewer's heart, and claimed him for a higher service. A severe struggle with old views and habits terminated in complete triumph, and he consecrated to the cause of Christ those energies which had been devoted to secular concerns. Uncle John abandoned his position in the brewery, and with it flattering prospects of wealth. He felt that it could be his calling no longer. "Heaven," I have heard him say, "seemed too far away when I looked up at it from among the beer barrels." Disengaged from worldly pursuits, he gave himself with zeal to tract distribution, exhortation, prayer-meetings, and various evangelical labors, so that the good people of P—— were astonished; many even thought him crazed. They did not understand the case. A mind of natural strength and fervency had received a strange and powerful impulse from new-born faith and love. To him, religious things, no longer invisible and distant, were seen and present. His awakened soul accepted Bible truths as living and wonderful realities. Christ's cross and judgment-seat seemed very near, radiant with tender attractions and with awful glories. The curtain concealing futurity had fallen; and from beholding the endless destinies of the righteous and the wicked, he turned to his fellow-men, and earnestly besought them to seek the divine favor and preparation for heaven.

This practical zeal for God and souls, arising partly from natural character and yet more from vivid realization of the truths of religion, was no temporary flame. Burning to-day with its original brightness, and with more than its original fervor, it is the immediate source of the ceaseless

Christian activity of our beloved Uncle John. He found but a limited sphere of usefulness in P——, and possibly had cause to feel that it was "his own country." Going westward, he spent some years traversing the prairies of Illinois with horse and wagon, as colporteur of the American Tract Society. God went with him over those grassy solitudes, and blessed his labors, and filled him with joy and praise. It was in this service that he gained that experimental familiarity with the best thoughts of Christian authors, and that wonderful command of religious language which have compensated in great measure for the want of a liberal education, and which have contributed greatly to his success in the work of the Lord.

Returning to P——, he began visiting the churches as Providence opened the door, and became instrumental of untold good in several wide-spread revivals. He went from place to place, "feeling his way" and working with the pastors. P—— county especially thrice witnessed a great outpouring of the Divine Spirit, chiefly in blessing upon his efforts. Finding an interest in some members of a decayed backslidden church, he would spend the day visiting in the congregation from house to house, conversing and praying with every one, and in the evening he would attend a prayer-meeting at the residence of some pious family; "for," says he, "it would never do to commence in a cold church; but after God pours down his Spirit in answer to prayer, then the lecture-room will be needed, and the church too." In those times his soul overflowed with happiness, when sanctuaries were nightly crowded with inquirers, and God came down in love and power.

As one of the almoners of the royal bounty of the Sanitary Commission, Uncle John is indefatigable. It is his special delight to find unseen and neglected spots, and to secure for them their share of comforts. Thousands of poor fellows bless him for timely and thoughtful care. Indeed I never met any one who combined in a similar degree prompt and exact attention to items of business with unremitting spiritual aims and efforts. It seems part of his religion to neglect nothing. Those evangelical labors, however, to which his other pursuits are subsidiary, are the chief exponents of his character and power. In these—I can express myself in no other way—in these Uncle John is *great*. His pleading particularizing prayers, his varied, choice, and ready store of hymns, his rapid yet unoffending directness of personal appeal, his easy and quick command of thought and language, his homely, pointed, and solemn method in public address, and his very appearance and voice and manner, unpretending and deferential, yet as earnest and sympathetic as they possibly could be--all qualify him to succeed anywhere, but especially with soldiers.

I have been amazed sometimes at the beauty of his prayers. On one occasion, during the heats of summer, we rode together through the woods to a distant pasture, that our horses, then fed only on grain, might enjoy grazing for an hour. Uncle John had been somewhat depressed, and we sat under the shade of a little tree. Suddenly he exclaimed, "Brother H——, let us pray," threw himself forward upon the grass, and instantly began, "O God, on this beautiful day, amid these old woods, and beneath thine own clear heavens, we lift up our souls to thee." His voice, at first slow and full, was rich with melody and pathos; and as petition after petition, exquisitely expressed, followed each other in beautiful succession, I thought the sacred eloquence of that unstudied prayer such as I had never heard before. While the prostrate body rested on hands and knees, crouching in lowliest humility, and the face, with close-shut eyes and intensity of expression, sometimes almost touched the ground, the longing, believing spirit seemed to rise, as on angels' wings, into the presence and glory of its God. While we were returning, he said that he seemed to have had a glimpse of heaven, and was refreshed and comforted. I could easily believe it.

Uncle John is a great power in a soldier's prayer-meeting, for he generally imparts to his fellow-worshippers much of his own spirit. With excellent wisdom he invariably looks to the chaplain for the organization and control of religious assemblies, even of those in which he himself may be the principal actor; "for," he says, "*I'm* nothing but an old shepherd dog, and I try to help the pastors in tending their flocks." But after the meeting has been set a-going, Uncle John, "assisted," as he would say, "by the good Spirit of the Lord," is the very life of it.

The first time I ever saw him was last winter, near B——, in a chaplain's meeting in the log church of the brigade. The quaint sprightliness, the overflowing brotherly love, the humility and Christian readiness of the little man, were apparent. Ever since the completion of the log chapel in our brigade, an increasing interest in religion had been manifested among the boys, and Uncle John promised to attend one of our meetings. He came, and moved us all by his earnest words and fervent prayers. After this I was going away for ten days, and asked him to look after my boys in my absence. He consented at once. On my return I was prepared for something of a revival, but not to learn that the chapel was crowded, and that meetings were kept up three times a day. And when I entered the chapel that afternoon, what a scene presented itself! The place was half Babel, half Bochim. Such a murmuring of confused sounds never before had greeted my ears. Most of the soldiers were kneeling by the benches, several were engaged in prayer, and sobbings and groanings, loud responses, and fervent ejaculatory petitions, resounded in every part of the building. Uncle John was in the midst of the congregation, kneeling in the aisle in front of the pulpit, and seemingly the most engaged of all. After the principal prayer was over, he rose, and in his sweet soprano voice began a favorite hymn; all joined; and the swelling praise went up through the white trembling canvas roof. Other prayers were offered, interspersed with verses of hymns and with remarks by Uncle John and the chaplain; and before the meeting was dismissed, all present were earnestly invited to attend the evening service. It seems that he had instituted the morning assembly for inquirers and young converts, and that in the afternoon for the prayers and exhortations of Christians generally, while more formal exercises occupied the meeting at night. The excitement and confusion at first seemed to me excessive and injurious; but I found that they were to a certain extent the natural consequences of religious feeling among the soldiers, and that they were rather checked than stimulated by Uncle John; for our soldiers sometimes remind one of those ancient warriors—"*homines rustici atque militares*"—whom Cicero mentions as having given vent to their enthusiasm in loud shouting. Besides, the other chaplains did not find the noise objectionable. The evening meeting was the most important. Generally there was regular service, including a sermon by one of the chaplains, after which those who loved the Lord and those who desired to do so, were requested to remain. Commonly very few went away; and then Uncle John's work began. After some prayers and hymns, he would make a short address, and conclude by asking those who felt themselves in need of salvation, and who desired Christians to pray for them, to stand up. And then what earnestness in persuading sinners to declare for Christ. He would continue making his remarks, and looking over the assembly, perhaps for a minute, till some one rose, "There's one," says Uncle John with visible emotion. "Oh, bless the Lord! There is joy in heaven over one sinner that repenteth." Then, after a short pause, he would add in the most inviting tones, "And is there no other precious soul here that wants a Saviour? Yes, there's another. God bless you, dear brother. Oh, it was for such that Jesus died—*Jesus* the SON OF GOD!" and Uncle John would sing,

"He died for you,
He died for me,
He died to set poor sinners free.
Oh, who 's like Jesus,
That died on the tree?"

Another pause. "And is n't there any more who want to love this blessed Saviour? Yes, I see you, dear brother. I knew there would be more. I feel that God is here to-night. And there's another, and another, and another. Oh, hallelujah! Praise the Lord!" Another pause. "Now come, dear friends; do n't be afraid. The Lord is waiting; and Oh, he is waiting to be gracious. You do n't suppose you're too great sinners to be saved, do you? The blood of Jesus Christ cleanseth from all sin. Yes, precious Saviour, precious Saviour, thy blood could cleanse a universe from guilt." In this way he would go on till perhaps a dozen or twenty had risen; after which, in order to intensify good resolutions, he would invite them to the front seats, which were vacated for them. This he did often, not always. After more prayers and hymns, the audience were dismissed, only the inquirers remaining; and then Uncle John and the chaplains conversed and prayed with each individual according to his case.

"Talking meetings," designed chiefly for remarks, exhortations, and relations of personal experience, sometimes took the place of these that I have described; they proved very useful. Uncle John participated in them, as he did in all the rest. The revival interest continued with little abatement for five or six weeks, and resulted in the establishment of small congregations of believers in those regiments that had chaplains. Nearly one hundred and fifty—about one-tenth of the whole brigade—professed faith in Christ, either renewedly or for the first time. Very few of these dear boys are with us now; many are in soldiers' graves; many are sick or wounded at home; some are in southern prisons, and some have finished their term and been discharged. But so far as I know, the great majority have shown that their profession was well-founded.

In all our meetings, Uncle John's singing did excellent service. To use an expression of his own, he is "a walking hymn-book." He has a large variety of hymns at command, set to appropriate tunes, and a wonderful faculty of instantaneously producing in a meeting the verses and notes specially suitable to each particular conjuncture. How often have I heard him, so soon as a prayer or address might end, strike up the hymn needed to correct or to carry out the impression of it. He would seldom sing the whole hymn; but if one or two verses satisfied the occasion, he would cease, that the meeting might go on. This tact often helped greatly to render the interest of our exercises continuous and progressive.

Uncle John's voice is not strong, but it is clear and pleasant; and as he sings with earnestness and truthfulness of expression, his lips sometimes seem to clothe old verses with new beauty, and to impart a striking and unexpected fulness of meaning to words that have long been familiar. Those who have heard him will not forget with what joyous faith he sings,

"Jesus shall reign where'er the sun
Does his successive journeys run;"

nor how invitingly and solemnly he renders

"There is a fountain filled with blood,
Drawn from Immanuel's veins;"

nor the tenderness of those lines,

"Come, trembling sinner, in whose breast
A thousand thoughts revolve;
Come with your guilt and fear opprest,
And make this last resolve;"

nor the heartiness of the verses,

"Come, ye sinners, poor and needy,
Weak and wounded, sick and sore;
Jesus ready stands to save you,
Full of pity, love, and power."

How boldly he raises that Christian battle-song,

"Am I a soldier of the cross?"

What thankfulness and love he puts into that grand hymn,

"Oh for a thousand tongues to sing
My dear Redeemer's praise!"

With what plaintive melody he sings,

"Did Christ o'er sinners weep?
And shall my tears be dry?"

and with what affectionate longing,

"Jerusalem, my happy home."

These and many other old hymns, and the tunes which accompany them, are weapons of power with Uncle John. Besides these, he has a collection of modern religious melodies, generally lively in character, and very popular with soldiers. Those beginning, "My heavenly home is bright and fair;" "There 's a light in the window for thee, brother;" "Must Jesus bear the cross alone?" "A beautiful land by faith I see;" and those which tell of the "Sweet hour of prayer," and of "The gospel ship," which is "sailing, sailing," and of "The heavenly shores" to which we are "homeward bound," are fair examples. They commonly have a chorus, which adds to their effect. I shall not soon forget the delight with which I first heard him singing a song, whose lively notes and cheerful rejoicing confidence accorded admirably with his own spirit. It was towards the close of a crowded meeting in the log chapel. He rose after a prayer, and turned round in the aisle so as to face the congregation. His right hand held the left by two fingers, and kept it out of the way behind his back. Standing in his humble but easy manner, he began in a clear voice,

"We are joyously voyaging over the main,
  Bound for the evergreen shore,
Whose inhabitants never of sickness complain,
  And never see death any more."

Warming as he went on, he kept looking over the audience to observe their feeling; and before he had finished, he was clapping his hands quietly in time to the tune, and leading us all in the chorus, like an enthusiastic singing-teacher. The hymn, though familiar now, was then new to most of us, but we could not help joining with Uncle John to the best of our ability in the chorus,

"Then let the hurricane roar,
  It will the sooner be o'er;
We will weather the blast, and we 'll land at last,
  Safe on the evergreen shore."

Few, perhaps none, went away from the meeting that night without resolving to secure transportation in that good ship, for which, according to his wont, Uncle John was looking up passengers.

Some striking qualities of Brother V——'s character are exhibited in his dealings with others relative to their religious state and duty. His earnestness of manner, his unfeigned and affectionate interest in one's personal welfare, and his entire freedom from any sort of conventionality or constraint, soon make the heart trustful, and beget openness of conference and confession. During a time of religious awakening, he labors with inquirers night and day. At B——, all who witnessed his zeal marvelled that flesh and blood could endure such incessant excitement and activity. Three meetings a day, in all of which he prayed and spoke and sang, seemed in no degree to diminish his energy for special and private exertions. For weeks he spent his spare time in going from tent to tent conversing and praying with every one who manifested any concern regarding religion. As he set out one morning to follow up the impressions of the preceding night, I went with him down into the company streets. Entering a tent where two out of the four occupants were Christians, he addressed himself to each man in suitable inquiries and exhortations, and led in a short prayer. Then he asked for a sergeant whom he knew to be under deep conviction. The young man came in as we were going out to find him. Uncle John instantly read the trouble of his face, which expressed the most profound melancholy; and laying his hand affectionately on the shoulder of the young man, exclaimed with sadness and tenderness, "O Albert, Albert, my dear boy, haven't you given your heart to the Saviour yet? What *is* the matter, Albert? Why don't you throw every thing else away, and trust only in the Lord Jesus?" The young man answered that he was trying to do that, but could not find any peace. Every thing seemed dark, somehow. Uncle John replied, "Then you must pray to God to make it light. *He* can cause light to shine in darkness. And now, dear boys, let us all pray for Albert, for nobody but God can help him, and let Albert pray for himself. Chaplain, lead us in prayer." We all knelt down in the little shanty, which barely held us. The chaplain prayed, and then Uncle John said, "Now, Albert, *you* pray." The lad offered a few simple and earnest petitions. We left him with some words of encouragement. Several days afterwards I met him going to one of the meetings with a shining and happy face. "Well, Albert," said I, "how do you feel to-day?" "Oh, bright as a shilling," was the singular but expressive reply; and bright ever since has been his Christian character and course.

Uncle John, without being exactly abrupt, is wonderfully quick and direct in personal appeal. His preparatory remarks, if he makes any, are very short; sometimes merely the manner and evident spirit of the man introduce what he says; but, in any case, the first startling sentence clears the way for any that may follow. "Here," said I, as we went down the street, "is Sergeant M——, Uncle John." "How are you, sergeant?" says the ready little man, taking the sergeant by the hand. "And I hope, chaplain, this good soldier has enlisted under the banner of King Jesus? Dear sergeant, how is it? Now just tell Uncle John. Are you trying to be a faithful servant of God? Have you given yourself to that blessed Saviour who died for you, and who bought you with his precious blood?" As these words were uttered with great earnestness and affection, the sergeant looked thoughtful. He confessed that he was not a Christian, but said that he often desired to be one. "Oh, why then delay? Why risk your eternity? Who knows how soon the whizzing bullet or bursting shell may lay one low? And then, to enter God's presence unprepared! Oh, sergeant, will you not seek the Lord now, and secure that glorious hope which is full of immortality?" With such words, spoken by the way, Uncle John has moved many a soul to the consideration of its eternal interests.

The treatment given to his approaches and exhortations by different parties is very various; but he is equal to any emergency. He instantly appreciates the nature of each case, and gives the instruction, encouragement, reproof, or reply which is needed. I have been astounded sometimes to hear officers, of whose profanity, drunkenness, gambling, and dishonesty, I was well aware, and who never to my knowledge showed even decent respect for religion, tell Uncle John that they were Christian men. I suppose they meant that they had been church-members while in civil life. They seldom deceived him. His interviews with such miserable men are generally made brief. Without even insinuating distrust, he utters a few awakening words, and is gone. "Oh," I have heard him say, "how solemn a thing it is to be called by the name of CHRIST. What a responsibility lies on us to adorn the doctrine of God our Saviour in all things; and how hard it is to be a Christian in *reality*, in deed as well as in name. Yes, dear friends, we must *strive* to enter in at the strait gate. I often think what a mercy it will be if Uncle John ever gets to heaven. It will be by the triumph of grace divine. Oh the riches of the grace of God!" With such sayings he leaves the backsliders thinking and ill at ease. Consistent believers, on the contrary, seldom meet him without enjoying some bright view of heavenly things, by which their hearts are strengthened in faith and hope and love.

The skill and spirit with which he replies to the pretences of unbelief and to the excuses of the unconverted, could not be surpassed. While maintaining the best temper, and exhibiting overflowing kindness and affection for souls, he attacks every form of sinfulness and error with unsparing fidelity. "O dear captain," I heard him say, "how I wish you would make up your mind to give yourself to the Lord Jesus Christ, and to become a faithful soldier of the cross." "Well, Uncle John," said the captain, "I try to do my duty, and I think that is all that is required of me." "Why, captain," answered the little man in tones of astonishment, "how *can* you say so? No man does his duty who does not give his heart to God, and live in God's love and service. What would you think of a man brought up by a kind father, and provided by him with every means of happiness, who should be a good brother and husband and neighbor and citizen, and yet be a heartless and undutiful son? Do n't you think his wickedness would be unspeakably great?" "But the cases are different," rejoins the captain. "No, they're not," said Uncle John. "That man would be condemned by the moral sense of the community; and the godless sinner, you may *depend* upon it, will be condemned by the public opinion of the universe." Thus boldly does this humble servant of God contend with the adversary, and assert the prerogatives of his Master; and he is as ready to do this with officers in high command as he is with private soldiers. Colonels and generals have received faithful admonition from him on things vital to their eternal peace.

On one occasion, I cannot say whether I was more amused to see the familiar yet respectful assurance, or gratified to witness the startling directness with which he interrogated a brave colonel whom he had never seen before. A meeting had been concluded in front of the head-quarters' tent, and Uncle John had conversed and prayed with a young man, who had shown deep conviction and anxiety regarding his sins. Utterly unconscious of human presence, and with a simplicity and earnestness which rose above all influences of time and place, and surrounded themselves with their own proprieties—silence, solemnity, and attention—he knelt with the lad in the midst of a crowd of bystanders, and prayed for him, for his comrades, for the officers of the regiment, and for the whole army. The vigorous colloquial language of the prayer, and its particularizing petitions, in which names and places and circumstances were freely mentioned, interested and impressed the hearers of it. Conventionalities plainly had little to do with Uncle John's religion. The young man went away comforted, and trusting in God; and the crowd dispersed. Then we entered the colonel's tent, in which we found one or two officers of the command, together with their chief. After a few words of conversation regarding the history of the regiment, and its part in the summer's campaign, in which it had lost heavily, Uncle John remarked that it was a blessed thing to have a hope that no bullet or cannon-ball can touch, and a life indestructible and immortal. Then turning to the colonel, he said in a confidential and coaxing way, "And now, colonel, just tell Uncle John, how it is with you. We are all perishing creatures, and must soon be in eternity together. Have you, dear colonel, a good hope in Christ? Can you say that you *know* that your Redeemer liveth? You'll pardon Uncle John for asking you; he's a poor dying old man that loves your soul, and wants it to be saved." This appeal, made rapidly, without any apparent premeditation, and with great tact and tenderness, evidently affected the colonel. Uncle John proceeded in the same manner as before, "You know what I mean. I don't mean, Are you a professor of religion? for there are many unworthy professors; but, has your heart been renewed by grace divine? That is the point. Have you become a new creature in Christ Jesus? Have you experienced that change of which our Saviour speaks when he declares that a man must be born again before he can see the kingdom of God?" The colonel expressed a hope that he was a Christian; and Brother V—— replied that he rejoiced to hear him say so; that he prayed the Lord to bless him and make him faithful to the end; and that he wished before God that all our leaders were earnest, believing men."

I have not spoken hitherto of Uncle John as a public speaker, because the peculiarities of his character are better illustrated by other topics, and perhaps also from a consciousness of inability to describe correctly his more sustained efforts. During the revival of last winter he frequently moved the audiences in the log chapel with short but thrilling strains of extemporaneous eloquence. Few of those who listened to these addresses regarded them in a rhetorical aspect; criticism is not in the line of soldiers; but all felt his power, and agreed that "he knew how to talk." Those of us, however, who were accustomed to notice mental methods, could not but wonder at the man's gifts. For myself, I listened to passages in his oratory such as, I think, are seldom heard from either pulpit or rostrum. His style at times reminded one of the more serious and moving utterances of Gough. But his discourses showed more argument than is commonly attempted in those of that interesting lecturer. Thought after thought was presented and illustrated with admirable though untaught adherence to the rules of art. The logical order of the ideas, their progressive continuity of impulse, their practical development and application, were faultless. Homely condensed language, natural and striking metaphors, unexpected similes, antitheses, and turns of expression, a becoming gesticulation, and a voice wonderfully persuasive and rich with sympathetic feeling, engaged attention, awoke the heart's best emotions, and excited new interest in the saving truths of Christianity. The sincere and humble earnestness of the man was also a chief element of his power. Not a word was uttered for oratorical effect. Every sentence manifested yearning love for souls, vivid conceptions of eternal things, and a solemn sense of the presence of God. Success too, though confidently looked for, was expected solely through the divine blessing. What wonder was it that such speaking produced results that have been visible ever since? For my part, I doubt not that it was instrumental of everlasting good.

During the early part of last summer he labored in the army of the James, among the colored regiments, and as might be conjectured, was very successful in arousing the lively African soldiers to the duties and attractions of religion. From one thousand to fifteen hundred souls were frequently present at meetings held in the open air. It was a scene worthy of a painter's skill, when the little man, in his own tender and telling way, addressed the gathered hundreds of his sable brethren; and when he led those assemblies in one of his stirring hymns, I think that the loud notes of praise rivalled in spirit and grandeur any that ever echoed from cathedral roofs.

After a time he was induced to have his headquarters with us, and to make our division the principal field of his labors. In this way I had the privilege, several times during the summer, of hearing him speak in public. His addresses are invariably extemporaneous. He says that deliberate composition is very difficult and irksome for him; which, indeed, might be inferred from his vivacious and emotional temperament, and his want of literary training. His efforts too, though always interesting to his hearers, are not always of equal power. I was particularly pleased with an address which he made one September evening in the plaza of Fort Davis to a regiment drawn up before him in line. The colonel had directed a notification of the companies for a prayer-meeting which we proposed to have; but the adjutant, thinking, I presume, to do the business thoroughly, ordered out the whole command, as if for dress-parade. Uncle John stood with his hands behind him, leaning against a tree in front of the headquarters, while company after company filed past him, faced to the rear, and dressed into correct position. The men evidently were wondering what was going on; and some of the officers seemed to think that a joke was being perpetrated on the chaplains and Uncle John. However we were ready for the emergency. A prayer-meeting was out of the question; so we resolved on some public exercises. After an introductory address, a hymn, and a prayer, Uncle John was invited to speak. He began by expressing his gratitude to the colonel for that opportunity of addressing the officers and men of "the dear old Seventh." He had come expecting only to attend a prayer-meeting, but was glad to meet so many brave men. As he looked on the faces before him, and saw how very few were present of those whom he had seen last winter, the thought arose, "Where were those brave boys that left the old camp at B——?" They are gone; they lie on the battle-fields of the Wilderness, and of Spottsylvania, and of the North Anna, and of Coal Harbor—all along the way from the Rapidan to Petersburg. Some are at home in the North, or in hospitals; but how many occupy their long, last home—a soldier's grave! Scarcely one is left of the familiar faces. Ah, well did he remember some of those noble boys that he used to see in the old log chapel, and whom he should see never more on earth. But, blessed be God, he had a bright hope of meeting them in heaven. They were heroes of Christ, and of his cross. Now they have fought their fight, they have finished their course, and they have received their crown. Oh, how he wished that every soldier was a truly Christian man, and prepared for any chance that might befall him. He knew many brave men who were not Christians; but it was always a mystery to him how any man could face death without a hope in that blessed Saviour, who had triumphed over death and the grave. He supposed a sense of duty would do much, but how much better was it to be sure that one's soul has been saved with an eternal salvation. Then the king of terrors is dethroned, and death becomes the gate of heaven. Did you never think, he asked, against what love you offend while you remain unreconciled to God? Oh, it filled all heaven with wonder when God's glorious Son took on him our salvation, and offered himself for our sins. Never was love like His love. How can you refuse your hearts to that loving, dying Saviour? Surely you will not suffer it to be that Christ should have died for you in vain.

"The Son of God in tears,
Angels with wonder see;
Be thou astonished, O my soul,
He shed those tears for thee.

"He wept that we might weep,
Each sin demands a tear.
In heaven alone no sin is found,
And there 's no weeping there."

Dear soldiers, if I know my own heart, I earnestly desire the welfare of you all. God knows that I love you, and want to see you happy. And when I think of the fatigues and exposures, and dangers which soldiers must undergo, Oh, how I wish to have them sustained and comforted by the hopes and consolations of the gospel! I would that every one of you had a sure title to a mansion in the skies. I would that you could all look from these scenes of conflict, and suffering, and death, to that blessed land where there is war no more. Oh, yes; no whistling minie ball, no bursting Parrot shell, shall disturb the peaceful inhabitants of that heavenly country. In that land there shall be rest for the weary; pain and grief shall not enter there;

"No groans shall mingle with the songs,
That warble from immortal tongues."

Now let me say a few words to those of you who are Christians. Dear brethren, you are surrounded by temptations; but strive to live faithfully; hold fast your profession; let no man rob you of your crown. Trust not in yourselves, but in One that is mighty. Keep looking up to Jesus, and you will be conquerors, and more than conquerors through him that loves you. Recently by the bedside of a dear corporal, that formerly belonged to your regiment, but that now sleeps in Jesus, I felt what truth, what power, there is in the religion of Christ. All was peace with him, perfect peace. He knew that he was dying; but he rejoiced in the hope of a better life, in the sure prospect of a glorious immortality. "Oh let me die the death of the righteous, and let my last end be like his." And as for you, dear friends, who are without Christ, will you not seek an interest in his salvation? Will you not begin to love and serve that Redeemer who can save and bless you for ever? Yes; Jesus is the Saviour that you need;

"None but Jesus,
None but Jesus
Can do helpless sinners good."

Oh, then, do not hesitate. To-morrow may be too late. Who knows how soon the bolt of death may come? Now, while it is called to-day, give your hearts to God, and kneel before him in penitence and prayer. Dear soldiers, I thank you for the kind attention with which you have listened to me. May the Lord bless you all, and bring you to his heavenly kingdom!

Such, as nearly as memory serves me, was the course of thought and style of language employed by Uncle John. But the foregoing sketch can give no adequate idea of the living power with which he spoke. His allusions to the uncertainty of life and the nearness of death had a peculiar significance with those whom he addressed. Several of their number had been instantaneously killed, not long before, on the picket line in front of the fort; and a day or two subsequently to our meeting, one poor lad was struck by a minie ball and died in five minutes, only a few paces from the spot where he had listened to Uncle John. The summer's campaign had made us all too much accustomed to these things.

Uncle John's labors during the summer with the sick and wounded of the army were abundant. He went with the trains and the steamboats laden with the disabled of the great battles, and exerted himself incessantly for the welfare of both body and soul. He considered no service too laborious or too menial to perform for the helpless sufferers. Many owe their lives to him, and by him many have been led into the way of life eternal. The large tents which constitute the hospital wards, receive daily visits from him; and any special want of their inmates engages his immediate attention. He is particularly ready to converse and pray with those who are dangerously ill, or who express spiritual anxiety. Every evening also, if duty does not call him elsewhere, he assists a chaplain in conducting short exercises. The wards, to the number of eight or nine are successively visited, and in each of them two or three verses are sung and a prayer is offered. In these services Uncle John's gift of song is most happily employed. His choice variety of hymns, his tact in selecting verses, and his admirable use of tunes, both old and new, contribute greatly to render this evening worship interesting and profitable. I have noticed, too, that occasionally he gives a line according to a version of his own, no way inferior to the variations of the hymn-books.

Besides these employments at the hospitals, a great part of his time is taken up in visiting the camps, where he distributes religious reading and sanitary comforts, and helps the chaplains at prayer-meetings and public services. These journeyings call into play his powers as a pedestrian, which are most extraordinary. He thinks nothing of a stretch of eight or ten miles; and one hot day of last summer I knew him to walk fifteen miles and back again, with very little appearance of fatigue. Everywhere, and among all classes, he finds a cordial welcome. Many chaplains particularly, and among them the writer of this, feel themselves under profound obligations to him; for we are generally agreed that it would be difficult, perhaps impossible, to find another man in the country so well qualified as he for religious labor among soldiers, at least for that kind of labor which Uncle John performs. And certainly no one could enter upon such work with more self-devoting zeal than that which animates this singularly-gifted man. The camp and hospital, the march and the bivouac, the siege-line and the battle-field, have witnessed his untiring energy in the service of a Divine Master. Ten thousand thanks to the American Tract Society for sustaining such a man in so blessed a work.

When I look upon Uncle John as he is now, a ready and mighty laborer in the cause of man's regeneration, and compare him with what he was sixteen years ago, the lively and driving manager of work in a brewery, I exclaim, "How powerful is the grace of God; what changes it can effect; how marvellously it fashions the most unlikely materials into blessed instrumentalities of good!" Under its influence, abilities and habits, developed in a life of eager worldliness, are employed with singular efficiency in the pursuit of heavenly objects; the want of early preparation and instruction is compensated by the improvement of a devoted mind; and a holy consecration of purpose is unflinchingly sustained for years, and crowned with ever-increasing success. Such an instance is rare; so that none should presume to squander precious time in the hope of future faithfulness; but what encouragement it contains for those, of whatever age or condition of life, who feel themselves called to some special department of the service of God. How surely he can sustain and prosper us while, in some fitting sphere, we labor earnestly for him!

I now bring to a close my intellectual companionship with Uncle John; and I do so with regret. It has pleasantly occupied some evenings, which otherwise might have passed unimproved in the bomb-proof and the wall-tent. Fare ye well, dear, good man. You have sometimes been a sad reproof to me for my want of resolution and fidelity in the discharge of a holy calling—a reproof none the less potent because all unconsciously administered: but for that I bear you no ill-will; I rather render thanks to Heaven that I have seen the living power of Christianity brightly illustrated, and I pray God for a baptism of his Holy Spirit, that I may more successfully emulate the example of his devoted servants, in closely following the footsteps of our divine Saviour. Fare ye well, dear Uncle John. May God long spare you, a blessing to your kind, and at last take you gently to his heavenly home! And when separating years shall have passed away; when the great war, now nearing its end, shall have been succeeded by times of national prosperity; when your friend, the chaplain, if God prosper him, shall have attained his desire, and be the pastor of some peaceful village flock; when your moving and persuasive voice shall be hushed in death; when your face and form, now welcome and familiar, shall present themselves no more for cordial greetings; and when your triumphant spirit, freed from earth's fetters, shall be rejoicing on high, in the activities of an immortal life—then it may give pleasure to review these pages, the souvenir of the acquaintance of a twelvemonth; to recall lovingly the most cherished memories of one's army life, and to think of a sainted Uncle John.

This remarkable man—John E. Vassa entered Richmond with the federal force upon its evacuation by the Confederates, and has ever since toiled with unflagging zeal, and amazing success, for the spiritual welfare of the Southern poor. Thousands of white and colored children have been taught to read God's word in Sabbath-schools formed through his agency; and hundreds of souls are blessing God to-day, that through him they have found Christ precious.

May he long live to serve that Saviour through Union Missionary Colportage as conducted by the American Tract Society!

www.ingramcontent.com/pod-product-compliance
Lightning Source LLC
LaVergne TN
LVHW011233110826
845150LV00006B/1622